AN
EDGE
IN THE
KITCHEN

AN
EDGE
IN THE KITCHEN

THE ULTIMATE GUIDE
TO KITCHEN KNIVES

How to Buy Them, Keep Them Razor Sharp,
and Use Them Like a Pro

CHAD WARD

WITH PHOTOGRAPHS BY
Bryan Regan

WILLIAM MORROW
An Imprint of HarperCollinsPublishers

HarperCollins books may be purchased for educational, business, or sales promotional use. For information please write: Special Markets Department, HarperCollins Publishers, 10 East 53rd Street, New York, NY 10022.

FIRST EDITION

Designed by Beth Tondreau BTD NYC

Library of Congress Cataloging-in-Publication Data has been applied for.

ISBN 978-0-06-118848-0

08   09   10   11   12   WBC/RRD   10 9 8 7 6 5 4 3 2 1

FOR MY WIFE, LISA,

who, for reasons known only to her,
puts up with this nonsense.

CONTENTS

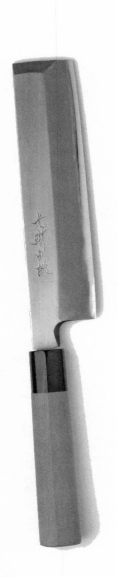

PART THREE: STAY SHARP 131

INTRODUCTION

Why write a book about kitchen knives? Because kitchen knives changed the world. Because they are the oldest and most important tool known to humankind. As Michael Symons wrote in *A History of Cooks and Cooking*, "The use of knives does not depend on culture, it *is* culture." If you include our prehuman ancestors, we have been using kitchen knives for about two and a half million years. That's a million years before fire became fashionable, just to put things into perspective. From those first crude stone edges to the sleek ultramodern hardware lining the walls of your local kitchen emporium, knives allow us to perform the most basic human task—preparing and sharing food.

Two and a half million years ago, *Homo habilis* ("handy man") first started chipping crude stone tools, including cutting edges. These tools played a significant role in the massive evolutionary changes that quickly followed. The ability to butcher and share scavenged meat, much richer in calories and nutrients than a strictly plant-based diet, led to rapid brain development, interdependent communal living, and improved communication skills. By the time the recognizably human *Homo erectus* hit the scene, they came equipped with big brains, advanced tools, and the small teeth that indicate a diet based on preprocessed (that is, cut-up) food. Puts your chef's knife in a new light, doesn't it?

The other reason for a book like this is the current culinary renaissance we are experiencing all over the world. We seem to have shaken off the perception of preparing meals as kitchen drudgery and embraced making and sharing food as something fun to do. Cooking is cool. And kitchen gear is even cooler. Those who are really into cooking—and those who would like to be—demand top-notch tools. Good knives are the cornerstone of any kitchen.

Despite our long history with knives, most of us are woefully uninformed about our kitchen knives. We are afraid to spend too much. Many of us are secretly afraid of them. We are intimidated by our knives when they are sharp, annoyed by them when they are dull, and quietly ashamed that we don't use them well and can't keep them sharp. That's a sad state of affairs for a species that has been using these things for nearly as long as we have been walking upright. Are we so familiar with kitchen knives that we have taken them for granted? Why is it that no one ever shows us how to use our knives properly? Or shows us how to keep them sharp? How do we know if we are buying the right knives? Can we buy good knives without breaking the bank? Should we get the ones that the famous TV chef uses? And why are chefs so obsessed with their knives anyway?

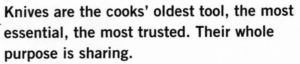

Knives are the cooks' oldest tool, the most essential, the most trusted. Their whole purpose is sharing.

—**MICHAEL SYMONS**, *A History of Cooks and Cooking*

This book is designed to answer some of those questions. *An Edge in the Kitchen* ties together illustrated step-by-step instruction with a little history, metallurgy, anthropology, kitchen science, and, I hope, a little humor. To make things easier, the book is divided into three basic sections: how to choose good knives; how to use them like a pro; and how to keep them razor sharp. But there is much more to know about kitchen knives than sharpening techniques and chiffonade. You will discover what a cow sword is (and why you might want one), why chefs are abandoning their heavy German knives in droves, and why the Claw and the Pinch, strange as they may sound, are in fact the way to make precision veggie cuts with speed and style. Along the way there are some interesting tidbits that show how kitchen knives have been shaped by cuisine and culture and vice versa.

THE AMERICAN SHUFFLE

One example of how knives have shaped culture is the unique American habit of switching the fork from the left hand to the right and back as we eat. Ever wonder why we do this awkward little move? It all came about because of a change in knife making in seventeenth-century France.

From the Middle Ages until the end of the 1600s, most diners ate with their fingers and a knife, which they brought with them to the table. Hosts and innkeepers didn't provide tableware. Except for the extremely wealthy who owned separate eating knives, these knives were used for everything from cutting rope to defending one's honor. These long, slender knives continued to be used as weapons and posed the conceivable threat of danger at the dinner table. However, once forks began to gain popular acceptance, there was no longer any need for a pointed tip at the end of a dinner knife to hold and spear the food. In 1669, Louis XIV of France decreed all pointed knives on the street or the dinner table illegal. The claim was that this would reduce violence. Other accounts of the story suggest that Cardinal Richelieu was so disgusted by his dinner guests constantly picking their teeth with tips of their knives that he had his house knives ground down. Others in the court followed suit and the king made it official.

By the beginning of the eighteenth century, knives imported to the American colonies had blunt tips. However, colonists were not shipped any forks, which were still somewhat exotic. Because Americans had very few forks and no longer had sharp-tipped knives to spear food, they had to use spoons in lieu of forks. They would use the spoon in the left hand to steady the food as they cut it with the knife in the right. They would then switch the spoon to the opposite hand in order to scoop it up to eat. This distinctly American style of eating continued even after forks became commonplace in the United States. ▲

As with many things in life, this book was born from failure. Many years ago I purchased my first real set of knives. This was back when dinosaurs roamed the earth (according to my kids), water was still free, and those of us with personal computers were astonished by Tetris in all its blazing 8-bit glory. The big-name German knives dominated the market. I knew a little about knives. I had cooked in restaurants throughout high school and college. Hefty Teutonic cutlery was what the real pros used, at least the trained chefs—line cooks used whatever garbage knives were on sale. A big block of high-priced steel from Solingen was what you bought when you wanted to announce to the world that you had arrived and were ready to cook, to prove that you were serious. So I did. And they were great. For a while.

I cooked for years with those knives, secure in the knowledge that I had purchased the finest kitchen cutlery on the planet. All the gourmet magazines said so. But I wasn't entirely comfortable using them and I couldn't keep them sharp. I tried steeling them like I'd seen chefs do, the blade clanging on the steel as I whipped the edge back and forth, which helped for a little while. I had them professionally sharpened, which was hit and miss, sometimes wonderful, sometimes disastrous. I took knife skills classes. I cooked a lot. I got better. A lot of reading and a lot of practice enabled me to sharpen my knives with a reasonable degree of skill. I could prepare a complex meal for guests without major blood loss. But I wanted more. I wanted to learn to use my knives like a pro.

I'm a writer by trade. I read a lot. I research. In between articles and assignments I tried to find some resource—short of a culinary degree—that would help me learn the skills I was looking for. There isn't much out there. The really scary realization is that once you start digging into the history, anthropology, physics, metallurgy, design, and manufacture of kitchen knives, you come to the startling yet inevitable conclusion that the vast majority of what we are taught about our knives (even in the most prestigious culinary schools) is either outdated or simply wrong. Classic knife techniques haven't changed over the years, but everything else has. There are better materials and better ways to make knives, there are better ways to use them, and there are better ways to keep them at peak performance.

On a practical level, *An Edge in the Kitchen* had its origin in a tutorial on kitchen knives I was invited to write for the online food site eGullet.org. I intended to dash off a quick article on maintenance and sharpening, but it turned into a 15,000-word polemic. The online class was well received. It seems that a lot of passionate cooks were looking for exactly that sort of information. But it became clear from the e-mails and questions I got back that there was still quite a bit of confusion, misinformation, and anxiety about kitchen knives. Above all, there was an almost frantic interest in *everything* there is to know about knives. Writing this book has allowed me to delve even deeper, to work with chefs and knife makers, to sort out the physics of edges and the trigonometry of sharpening, to figure out what works and what doesn't, and put it together in a way that anyone can use. If you can stack blocks, you can cut restaurant-quality diced vegetables. If you can fold a paper airplane, you can sharpen your knives better than many professionals. If you are willing to do some shopping around, you can find modern kitchen knives that outperform anything ever produced. In short, with just a little knowledge and a little hands-on practice, you can gain a serious edge in the kitchen.

Knives are simple tools. A well-made knife resonates on a primal level.

—BOB KRAMER, ABS Master Bladesmith

Part One
CHOOSE YOUR WEAPON

What makes for a good knife, and how do you make an intelligent choice from the yards of glittering steel at the kitchen store? More important, can you do it without missing a car payment?

Absolutely. While you can indeed spend nearly $5,000 on a hand-forged sashimi knife (and I have a couple to recommend), you can also outfit your first kitchen with quality knives for less than $50. The trick is to know what is *really* important when buying knives—and it isn't the "full tang and bolster" marketing drivel that every kitchen store "expert" seems legally required to rattle off. This section will teach you what to look for when shopping for knives. It will also cover the basic knife types and their uses—including what that weird little curved knife in the display cabinet is* and why you shouldn't be a blockhead. And because it is vital to know how to accessorize, we also will cover the importance of a proper cutting board (and why those people who use glass boards are going straight to hell).

*HINT: The curved knife is a bird's beak paring knife. It is used to tourné vegetables into seven-sided footballs. Why? No one knows except the French, and they glare at you if you ask.

SO YOU WANNA BUY A KNIFE

Buying a good knife or two can be a little like buying your first car. It seems intimidating and expensive. There's a lot of mumbo jumbo and very little clear information. There are a lot of people with a lot of very strong ideas about what you should want, need, and desire. Some of them even have good intentions. Very few of them are unbiased and objective.

Much of the problem comes from well-meaning teachers and writers who just haven't kept up with what's going on in professional kitchens, much less metallurgy labs, knife makers' workshops, or manufacturing facilities. It's much easier just to repeat what has been written before or what is taught in an introductory knife skills class. If a prestigious culinary school teaches something, it must be true, right?

No. While certain knife skills are timeless, knife technology isn't. We've put a dune buggy on Mars, yet many knife skills teachers are still clinging to fourteenth-century technology and beliefs. The advances in knife steels, knife production, sharpening methods (based on actual science and experience—what a concept), and kitchen gear make the "common knowledge" about kitchen knives look like medieval dentistry.

There are several myths about knives that you'll find in nearly every weekend knife skills class, magazine article, and online resource. I'm sure you've heard them by now:

- You need an array of knives to deal with all of the jobs in the kitchen. And of course you'll need a *knife block* to keep them in.
- You must buy a *forged* knife. Forged knives are far superior to cheap, stamped knives.
- A heavy knife is better than a lightweight knife. A heavy knife will do the work for you.
- A good knife will always have a *full tang.* In a quality knife, the handle slabs will be *riveted* to the tang.
- A solid *bolster* is a sign of quality. It's there to balance the knife and keep your fingers from slipping onto the blade.

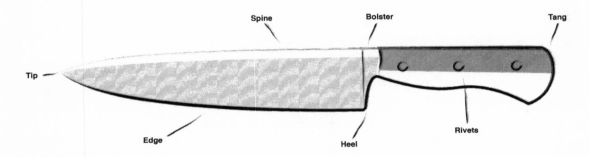

Each and every one of these pieces of advice is outdated, outmoded, or just dead wrong. Like the "sear meat to seal in the juices" myth that has persisted since a German chemist dreamed it up in the sixteenth century, these knife myths persist in spite of the evidence and in spite of the experience of cooks, knife makers, metallurgists, engineers, and anyone who has ever stood in front of a cutting board for several hours dicing apples or cutting winter squash. Let's knock them down one by one by one.

WHAT DO YOU REALLY NEED?

So, what do you *really* need? I use a chef's knife for everything. (I recognize that with forty-three chef's knives on hand at the moment, I may not be a representative sample.) Truthfully, with a good chef's knife and a paring knife you can do anything and everything you ever need to do in a kitchen. Throw in a big serrated bread knife and you'll own the world. Anything else is a convenience rather than a necessity.

> **Knives are fundamental. They are the first and most important tool in the kitchen. You need two, a big one and a little one. They must be sharp.**
>
> —MICHAEL RUHLMAN, author of *The Elements of Cooking*

Sounds like heresy, doesn't it? All of your friends have big blocks full of fancy knives, so that's what you want, too. Fine, you *might* want to expand beyond the Big Three, especially if you share your kitchen with someone else or if you do a lot of specialty cooking that would be easier with a dedicated style of knife. Or, like me, you might just really like kitchen knives and want to own a bunch of them. I'll clue you in on what's worthwhile and what is just filler. To start, how do you go about choosing your knives? More importantly, how do you *not* choose your knives?

Don't Be a Blockhead

You see them in the store. They are beautiful, with their sexy handles all lined up just so. You glance around and then surreptitiously fondle them, damning the safety device that keeps you from sliding the gleaming blade from the block. The salesman sidles up and in a throaty whisper says, "It comes with the sharpening steel *and* the mango slicer." You swoon. A mango slicer? Who knew there was such a thing? This must be a great set of knives.

Thus you are seduced. And like all victims of seduction,

you know that not all is as it seems, but you don't care. You buy the big block of knives. It's a steal! You got nine knives, some kitchen shears, and a sharpening steel for the same price as just two knives down at the high-rent end of the store display. Thus begins a cycle of frustration and recrimination that will *still* leave you using just three knives. Three mediocre knives. Three knives that you don't like and aren't comfortable using. Three knives that will sit forlornly in the block with their unused siblings when you can't take it anymore and upgrade to better knives.

So, don't be a blockhead. Don't buy knives you don't need. Buy fewer, higher-quality knives and build slowly. Mix and match to suit your tastes and cooking styles. You'll be happier. Yes, you say, but with the set I also get a handy block to store my knives in. Yep, you do. Are you sure it's the block you want and need? Will it hold your knives when your tastes change or you come home with an exotic new knife? Probably not. We'll explore storage options a little later. Rest assured, we won't leave your knives without a good home.

> **For a cook, knives are the most important tool in the kitchen—head and shoulders above anything else but the stove. Even when you have a bunch of knives in the block there are certain knives that you will always reach for.**
>
> —RUSS PARSONS, *LA Times* columnist and author of *How to Pick a Peach*

Back to that set of knives. Buying knives is very much like buying a good home entertainment system. You can indeed purchase everything together in a convenient set—probably packaged with a handy, dandy cabinet to put everything in—but as any audiophile or home theater buff worth his hundred-dollar speaker wire will tell you, different manufacturers have different strengths. One may make great speakers, another may make wonderful DVD players but lousy amps or receivers, and none of them makes a cabinet that fits the style of your room. Play to each maker's strengths.

You might like a big, heavy chef's knife from one manufacturer but find their carving knife too short for your tastes. If you eat a lot of veggies, you might like a thin Japanese vegetable knife. Are you a bread lover? Then a truly great bread knife is a must, and the ones that come with most sets are nearly useless. If you enjoy Asian-style cooking, you might be able to do everything you ever need with a single Chinese cleaver. Really think through what you want in your knives and buy only what suits your tastes, cooking style, and budget. Don't buy more than you need right now. Get the best you can afford and start slow. We will take a thorough look at a wide variety of knives and examine how they are made and what to look for. Then you will be in a better position to figure out what works best for you. And they don't have to match. Mismatched handles in the knife block or kitchen drawer are a sign of a comfortable and self-assured cook.

In other ways buying a big block of knives is like buying one of those sets of leather-bound classic books. You know, the "timeless works of literature, poetry, philosophy, and history" guaranteed to fill at least six feet of bookshelves or your money back. You get a couple of shelves full of books, but you don't have any control over what ends up in your library. You may indeed receive a couple of true classics. You might even get an obscure work of absolute genius—but don't count on it. What you really are buying is homogeneity and the promise that if you buy the matching set you'll look like you know what you're doing.

That block of knives looks great to the uninitiated, but it doesn't do anything to address what you—and you alone—really want or need as a cook.

With today's lifestyles, we never have enough time. Pick one very good knife and learn to use it well. You don't have time to fool around.

—MARTIN YAN, cookbook author and host of
Yan Can Cook

Don't Panic

If you already have a nice matched set of knives, don't despair. I'm not condemning the knives themselves, just the marketing hype behind them. We can tweak and tune what you have into hot-rod performance. You won't believe that these are your knives anymore. And when you start using them like a pro, you'll be giddy. Promise.

IF YOU ABSOLUTELY HAVE TO BUY KNIVES AS A SET

Okay, you say, but what if I'm buying these knives as a gift? I want to buy everything they need. I want to show them how much I care. I want to show them how much I spent.

Or maybe you just really, really like the look of a matching set of knives in a factory block.

Fair enough. If you do indeed need to buy a set of knives all at once, find a specialty cutlery store or gourmet kitchenware shop. The large department stores don't have the leeway to do what we're going to do next: mix and match within a set. A good specialty store sees the prepackaged set as a starting point. They carry all or most of the knives in open stock anyway, so they're willing to let you trade, say, the wholly inadequate 6-inch chef's knife that comes with many sets for a more suitable 8-inch or 10-inch length. They put the 6-inch knife back in the display cabinet and you pay the difference. Or you could make up the difference by dropping the tomato knife altogether. Dump the too-short bread knife and replace it with a 10-inch one. And for God's sake, get rid of the "sharpening" steel. If you are forced to keep the steel, advise your gift recipients to foist it off on someone they hate. In the meantime, get them a good high-grit ceramic honing rod to take its place. If the shop doesn't have a ceramic rod from that manufacturer, swap the coarse steel with the most finely grooved steel available. It's usually labeled Fine or Super Fine and is available from all major manufacturers.

If the shop isn't willing to do this for you, find another store or check the resource section in the back of the book. The Internet and mail order are the great retail leveling tools. Someone out there will be happy to accommodate you.

The reason for these choices will be revealed shortly. In the meantime, you have a solid basic set of great knives: a minimum 8-inch chef's knife, a 3- to 4-inch paring knife or two, a minimum 10-inch bread knife, and a high-grit ceramic honing rod. It all fits nicely in the gift-wrappable box. You are a genius and a loving person who wants only the best for the happy and clueless recipients (who probably won't even send a thank-you note). Come to think of it, these knives are too good for them. Go with the toaster instead. ▲

COMMON KNIFE MYTHS

Let's deal with the three biggest myths and misconceptions about quality knives: forging, bolsters, and full tangs, or, the Historical Fiction, the Convenient Fiction, and the Outright Lie.

Stamp of Approval

Nearly every piece of advice that involves knives contains some variation on the idea that forged knives are superior to stamped knives, conjuring up images of a burly artisan lovingly whacking a glowing bar of steel into your soon-to-be-purchased knife. Conversely, stamped knives are presented as being punched, cookie cutter style, out of thin, cheap steel. Old World hand craftsmanship versus crass automated garbage.

The real world is not that simple. If you compare a hundred-dollar forged knife from the gourmet boutique to the stamped knife you picked up at the grocery store in an emergency, forged knives do come out way ahead. But that's about the only time the myth is true. The fact is that in a modern manufacturing facility, stamped knives aren't really stamped and forged knives aren't really forged, at least in the way we normally think of those terms.

But wait, you say, I've read that forging aligns the molecules of the steel and makes it stronger. It also refines the grain structure, making for better steel. Forged knives are heavier, and that's better, right? And they have that bolster for balance and safety, you cry. Stamped knives are flimsy and icky.

First, a Little Terminology

For the sake of this discussion, I'm going to dismiss the cheapo stamped knives. There is a sea of stamped knives out there. Some are decent knives, some are garbage, but they are, in fact, made by punching a knife shape out of a flat sheet of steel and putting a simple edge on it. They tend to be very inexpensive and very light. Some have such a low carbon content that they will never take or hold a working edge. Their handles are usually molded plastic and they never have bolsters. For the most part, you can ignore them. There *is* one inexpensive stamped knife that I like a lot for starter kitchens and we will discuss it when we get to that section. The rest aren't worth bothering with, even the ones from reputable manufacturers who have gotten into the low-end market. Later on we'll take a look at the warning signs so you know what to avoid.

The knives we're *really* talking about here have been taking the professional cooking world by storm for the last several years and they are starting to make headway into the home market. You may have seen knives by Global or MAC infiltrating your local Gourmet Hut. They are good examples of this new type of knife. The blades are cut and precision ground from a billet of high-alloy steel, a method that custom knife makers refer to as "stock removal." They are indeed laser cut or punched from a sheet or thin bar of steel, but the level of finish that goes into them is equal to any of the forged knives. In fact, the manufacturing process is nearly identical.

I think of them as *machined* knives to distinguish them from stamped knives. Professional chefs have been abandoning their heavy forged knives (and repetitive stress injuries) in droves for this style of knife.

Three 10-inch chef's knives: machined, forged, stamped.

Bring On the Heat

The method of shaping the blade of a quality modern chef's knife is largely irrelevant. Why? Heat treatment. Take two pieces of the same steel. Grind one to a given shape and forge the other into the same shape. At this point in the process, forging does impart all of those wondrous virtues you've read about. There *is* a difference in the internal structure of the two knives, and the forged blade is indeed better. Sounds pretty good so far, doesn't it? But we still have a ways to go before we have a finished knife. Any difference between the two chunks of steel is wiped out in the next step: heat treatment, one of the most important aspects of creating a quality knife.

Heat treatment? Is that some kind of spa bath for your knife blade? Well, sorta. And as it turns out, it's all about the heat, baby. Give those two knife blades the same heat treatment and the steel will be identical. You wouldn't be able to tell them apart unless you have a scanning electron microscope in your kitchen.★ Since they have the same shape, they function exactly the same. One method takes a steel blank and grinds away everything that doesn't look like a knife. The other takes a steel blank, heats it up, and squishes it into the shape of a knife. Once they have been heat treated, that's the only practical difference.

Here's how it works. Knife steel is deliberately left soft during most of its manufacturing. It's easier to shape, cut, and

★ Yes, for you metallurgists out there, there would be a very slight difference in the directionality of the grain of the steel, but it's not something that's going to affect the performance of a knife blade, especially in the kitchen.

grind that way. One of the last steps before the steel blank gets fluffed and buffed into a real knife is a soak somewhere between 1,400 and 1,900 degrees Fahrenheit, which causes a radical change in the crystal structure of the steel. When cooled rapidly—"quenched"—the crystal structure changes again, creating an extremely hard, very brittle steel. It is under enormous internal strain. Think fourteen cups of coffee and an impending mortgage payment. That kind of pressure. Ready to shatter at the slightest provocation.

The knife blank is then heated again to a much lower temperature, somewhere between 400 and 700 degrees Fahrenheit, to ease some of the internal strain a little, making the steel slightly softer (though still much harder than it was initially) and a lot less brittle. At this point, all of those internal changes have wiped the atomic Etch A Sketch clean. Any advantages of the forged knife have been erased. That's if the two knives started out from the same steel. And as we'll see, some modern stamped knives take advantage of seriously vicious high-tech alloys.

Where did this idea of creating a superior blade by forging come from? For centuries forging wasn't just a way to make better steel, it was the *only* way to make steel. That's why I refer to this myth as the Historical Fiction. Now, knife makers no longer have to melt their own iron ore and pound it into submission. They simply call the steel mill and order up a batch. There is some great steel out there now, better than anything ever before used for kitchen knives. It can be drop-forged or it can be laser-cut out of sheets. With proper heat treatment, the method of shaping the blade has more to do with manufacturing processes and knife styles than anything else.

So why all the hype about forged knives? It's a great way to sell knives, for one thing. For another, the forging process is more labor-intensive and expensive. No one is going to go to that much trouble to make a lousy knife. Forged knives are good; they're just not inherently better. At least not better than the modern crop of machined knives out there. That's where the myth falls down. As I said before, if you compare a hundred-dollar forged knife with a cheap grocery store knife, the forged knife wins. No contest. But put that same forged knife up against a similarly priced knife ground from a billet of modern *uber*steel and properly heat treated and you've got an entirely different outcome. There is no clear winner. Each method can produce great knives, but they are knives with wildly different characteristics. You've got a choice to make.

Forged versus Stamped, Round 2: The Real Story

Forged knives and machined knives tend to be made in two distinctive styles. The forged knife generally will be thicker and heavier. This can be a good thing or not, depending on what kind of cooking you do. Many cooks like a heavy knife. The machined knife will be thinner and lighter.

The forged knife will generally have softer steel. Soft is a relative term when you are talking about steel. It *is* steel, after all, but it hasn't been heat-treated to optimal hardness. The softer steel can easily be resharpened at home, but won't hold an edge as long or take as acute an edge as harder steel. The machined knife will generally have harder steel. It will take an extremely keen edge and hold it for a good long time. It will be more difficult to resharpen (unless you read my chapter on sharpening your knives).

The forged knife will have a heavy bolster, the collar of metal between the handle and the blade. The bolster will probably extend most or all of the way down to the heel of the knife. The machined knife may or may not have a bolster. If it does, the bolster will have been welded on rather than forged into shape. Either knife may or may not have a full tang. We'll get to bolsters and tangs in just a minute.

So it's really more a matter of style and feel than quality. Some chefs like a heavier knife with a thicker blade, the type of knife that has been in vogue, at least in Europe and countries influenced by European (read: French) cooking, for a couple of hundred years. Other cooks like a thinner, lighter knife that feels more nimble in the hands and doesn't leave them feeling like they've been powerlifting all afternoon. This style of knife is heavily influenced by Japanese knives, known for their light weight, hard steel, and screaming sharp edges.

The truth of the matter is that unless you are in a production kitchen (where you're likely to be handed whatever knife was on sale when the kitchen was equipped), it comes down to a matter of feel. Remember, we're not dedicated to having knives that are all alike. We can mix and match. Make your decision based on what feels right in your hands, in your kitchen, and on your wallet rather than any fictional virtues of a particular manufacturing process.

Speaking of fiction . . .

Bolster BS

The traditional argument is that the bolster, that thick collar between the blade and handle, adds weight and balances the knife. Both of those are true. Whether or not that's a good thing depends on how you like to use your knife. The idea is to put a little weight behind your fingers when you grip the knife with a chef's Pinch grip. The bolster, combined with the weight of the tang and handle material, counterbalances the weight of the blade. I happen to like my knives to be a little blade-heavy, so a bolstered knife that shifts too much weight behind my fingers feels awkward and slightly out of control. It's all a matter of feel and preference. A bolster does provide a nice transition point and can help keep moisture and crud from getting onto the handle.

Contrary to the marketing brochures and the oh-so-helpful display down at the Towels'n'Such ("full bolster for safety!"), the bolster is not a finger guard, at least not on a chef's knife. Any knife with the blade heel lower than the handle has just as much protection for your fingers as a bolstered knife. The bolster does not prevent your hand from slipping forward onto the blade—the difference between the blade height and handle does that. The term butchers use is "stubbing." That's when the tip of your knife hits something hard, forcing it to a sudden stop and causing your hand to slide forward onto the blade. You can cut yourself badly this way. However, it is really only a problem on knives with blades the same width as the handle or narrower—a boning knife, for example. That style of knife does need some sort of extension below the handle as a safety feature. A chef's knife, though, has a blade significantly taller than the handle. Stubbing is nearly impossible. A chef's knife does not need a bolster, especially not one that extends down to the heel. That style of bolster will either keep you from using the full length of your knife's edge or lead to the premature death of your knife.

The bolster is—or at least used to be—the sign of a forged knife, which leads us back to the "stamped versus forged" argument above. Nowadays, stamped knives are just as likely to have bolsters welded on because that's what the marketing department and the general public think a knife should look like. To be fair, a bolster does add an element of polish and finesse to the look of a knife. In fact, if a manufacturer makes more than one line of knife—a budget line and a luxury line, for example—they will frequently put bolsters on the higher-end knives as a way to distinguish them from the cheaper knives. Bolsters add heft and a certain gravitas to things. Like a cummerbund.

Top to bottom: Forged chef's knife with partial bolster, forged French knife with older-style ferrule bolster, and modern machined chef's knife with welded-on bolster.

In addition to everything that the bolster doesn't do, what a bolster *does* indisputably do is make sharpening your knives a serious pain in the butt. It also keeps you from using the heel of the knife effectively. If you've seen a chef's knife that has been sharpened on an electric sharpener for any length of time, you'll notice a scooped out area just forward of the heel that keeps the knife edge from sitting flat on the cutting board. The same thing happens with any sharpening method; it's just generally more obvious with electric sharpeners.★ The collar itself is not the problem, but when the bolster extends down the back portion of the knife toward the heel, it causes the edge to ride up during sharpening, changing the angle. Do this long enough and you'll dish out a portion of the edge just forward of the heel and whole lot of metal will have to be removed to get your knife back into serviceable shape. At least one manufacturer of high-end forged cutlery, Chef's Choice, grinds its bolsters flat at the heel for this very reason. Wüsthof and Messermeister both offer lines of knives with the bolster extending only partway down the blade back. Most machined knives either don't have bolsters or only have a collar between the handle

★In the sharpening section, I'll show you how to avoid this problem.

and blade. Either type makes the knife much easier to sharpen. These are the only kinds of bolster I can recommend in good conscience.

The myth of the bolster is a Convenient Fiction: Call it a feature and claim it's a sign of quality. Clever. Luckily most professional knife sharpeners offer a bolster reduction service. Think of it as liposuction for your knives. It puts them back in fighting trim so they can be sharpened and used to their full potential.

And now to the Outright Lie . . .

Sharp and Tangy

The tang is the tongue of metal that extends from the blade backward. It is where the handle is attached. A full tang is the same size and shape as the handle slabs and is sandwiched between them. In direct contradiction to nearly 9,000 year s of metal knife and sword making, many knife manufacturers claim that you absolutely must have a full tang for your knife to be any good. You don't. A full tang is pretty, but hardly necessary, especially not in the kitchen.

Full Tang

Let's look at this logically. Metal is expensive and hard to work. You don't waste it and you don't pound it more than you have to, at least you don't when you don't have power tools. That's why knives and swords from the justly famous Japanese *katana* to the Viking *scramasax* to the American Bowie knife had stick tangs or rattail tangs hidden inside the handle. These are hard use blades, designed to cut through rope, leather, armored people, and just about anything or anyone that needed cutting. The tang was a place to attach a handle. As long as it was long enough to provide proper leverage, it was fine. Same with your chef's knife.

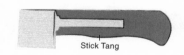

Stick Tang

In fact, it wasn't until after World War I that a full tang and slab handles even became practical, much less desirable in the kitchen. Stainless steel was introduced in England in

1914,★ but it took several years to work the kinks out (well, that, and there was that pesky world war to deal with). Until that time, and for quite a while afterward, knife blades were made of carbon steel. Carbon steel rusts and corrodes readily. The last thing you want is a way for moisture and goo to get inside the handle. That's a big reason hidden tangs were de rigueur—there was only one entrance point, the juncture between the blade and handle. A full tang with riveted handles provides the equivalent of valet parking all the way around the perimeter of the handle for crud to work its way between the tang and slabs. In fact, there is a school of thought that says the modern, injection molded handle with a hidden tang is more sanitary for this very reason.

Unless you are planning to jack up your car or pry open doors with your chef's knife, the tang plays little or no role in its strength and durability. It does help establish the balance and feel of the knife, but as we discussed with bolsters, there are many ways to balance the knife. With modern manufacturing methods, it is inexpensive to place riveted handle slabs on a full tang. A full tang is a manufacturing choice and a stylistic choice. If you like them, great, have at it. Just keep in mind that any reasonably sized tang that extends at least two-thirds of the way into the handle will be fine.

If you insist on a full tang, you'll miss out on a huge array of truly spectacular knives. Want to spend a couple of thousand dollars on a custom-made Japanese *yanagiba* (sashimi knife) hand-forged by a master craftsman with a 700-year history of knife making behind him? Oops, can't do it, the yanagiba has a stick tang. Want a reasonably priced chef's knife that won't expire if it finds its way into the dishwasher every once in a while.† Sorry. Hidden tang. You're out of luck.

★By some accounts, chromium steel was first developed in America in 1865 or 1871 (depending on the source) by a guy named Julius Bauer, but it didn't catch on, largely because it was too difficult to work.
†Yes, this is a very bad idea. I am aware, however, that it happens. No one dies.

A BIT OF HISTORY

Full tangs became popular during the Industrial Revolution when water- or steam-powered trip-hammers and drop forges made mass-produced knives affordable. In New England in 1830, John Russell put his fancy new machinery to work drop-forging punched-out hunting and skinning knives for the booming westward expansion. Settlers could hardly afford the expensive, hand-forged hunting knives that were the standard until then. Drop forges could quickly bang a knife shape out of a blank. Powered machines punched holes in the tangs so that scale handles could be attached, a more automated and cheaper method than attaching handles to hidden tangs, which had to be done by skilled craftsmen. ▲

The tang should be pretty far down on your list of things to look for when choosing a knife or two to outfit your kitchen.

It might seem like I don't like traditional forged, bolstered, full-tang knives. Not true at all. I like them very much. What I don't like is half-truths that mislead the buying public into thinking that because those features are part of a quality knife, that all quality knives must have those features. That's like saying that because some of the finest cars available are convertibles, any car that isn't a convertible must be inferior. The argument just doesn't hold up. It's a big old world out there. People's tastes and needs are different.

FEEL, STEEL, AND ANOTHER WORD THAT DEFINES CUTTING ABILITY (AND IN A PERFECT WORLD WOULD RHYME WITH THE FIRST TWO)

Now that we have taken several of the sacred cows of kitchen knifedom and turned them into tartare, what do you really look for in a kitchen knife? Let's start with the basics, the things that apply to every knife in your kitchen. Then we'll move on to specific knives and knife styles.

See Me, Feel Me

First and foremost, feel. A knife has to feel good in your hands. The most expensive knife in the world isn't worth much if you never take it out of the rack because it is uncomfortable to use. Feel is a very subjective thing. Handle contour and width, the weight of the knife, how it balances in your hand—all of those affect how a knife will feel to you. Unfortunately, there is no simple test. A lot of people will check the balance of a chef's knife by laying it flat across their forefinger just in front of the bolster and seeing if the blade and handle are the same. That's fine if you like your knives that way. I don't. I prefer my knives to be weighted forward. I feel like that gives me more control and precision.

Knife handles come in a variety of shapes and styles, from traditional Japanese wooden handles to high-tech ergonomic marvels. The right handle is the one that feels good to *you*.

While every manufacturer touts its steel, its pedigree, or its out-of-the-box sharpness, nobody says much about handles, probably because handles are personal and hard to quantify. I like mine as simple as possible—just give me the basic squared or oval handle, please. I do have a knife with an octagonal handle for times when I'm feeling sporty. I don't like handles with "ergonomic" humps, bumps, or finger grooves. They always feel like they were designed for some three-fingered alien with much bigger hands than mine. Something like that, though, might fit your mitts perfectly. At the very least, the handle should be comfortable and smooth. There shouldn't be any rough edges or transition points that feel pokey or sharp. The ideal handle would feel as rounded and smooth as a well-used bar of soap. I have yet to meet this mystical ideal handle, but that's what we're shooting for. Check where the blade meets the bolster (if it has one). The seam should be, well, seamless. If the knife has a riveted handle, check to make sure the rivets are flush. Hold the knife in a Pinch grip (see illustration). Does the spine feel like it's cutting into the base of your finger? If it does, this knife is going to be very uncomfortable to use for any length of time. You will eventually build up a callous if you use your knives a lot. All cooks do, but there is no reason to go through undue pain and suffering.

After handle feel come weight and balance. I like knives that are balanced a little forward of the blade-handle joint so they feel like they're tipping down when you hold them. Other people like a more neutral balance. I find that a blade-heavy knife gives me more leverage when powering through a pumpkin but balances nicely when held in a Pinch grip with my forefinger and thumb just forward of the blade-handle juncture. Folks who like neutrally balanced knives tend to favor bolsters because the bolster adds weight to the handle of the knife and counterbalances the blade. I don't mind bolsters as long as they don't interfere with sharpening, but I don't find them an advantage to the way I prep for dinner. Smaller knives are going to be balanced a little differently than larger chef's knives and slicers, but they still have to feel right in your hands.

Blade length and width are also personal choices and affect how you use a knife. In a chef's knife, a wide blade is handy for scooping up the stuff you've just cut. However, wide blades are intimidating to some people, sometimes without them even realizing why. The same person who was fine using a narrow 10-inch slicing knife may balk at a wide-bladed 10-inch chef's knife. It just looks too big to them. There *can* be something intimidating about that much pointy real estate. At one time I owned a custom-made 10-inch chef's knife that, at 3 inches wide, seemed more suited for bludgeoning oxen than fine-dicing brunoise. If you ever need to gut a T-Rex, I've got the knife for you. I sold it to another cook and kitchen knife aficionado who thinks it's the greatest thing ever. De gustibus non est disputandum and all that.

If you like to cook, you probably already have an inkling of what you do and don't like about the knives you've used in the past (or even the ones you are using now). Give it some thought. Better yet, get yourself down to your local cutlery boutique and try out a couple of knives. A good knife shop or kitchenware store will allow you to see how a knife feels in your hands. A really good one will have a cutting board on hand so that you can test drive the knife a little before whipping out your credit card. Shop around. Do a little hands-on research. You are spending your hard-earned money on something that will last you the rest of your life. Take your time. If you don't live near a cutlery store, there are several knife vendors on the Internet who have reasonable return policies if you hate the way a knife you've mail-ordered feels. This way takes a little longer, but opens up a huge array of possibilities.

WHAT TO WATCH OUT FOR

So how do you determine which knives are worth your time and money? Sometimes it can be a little hard to tell, especially if this is the first time you are in the market for a quality knife or two. Here are the warning signs that the knives you are looking at might not be all that they seem:

- Locale: You generally don't find quality kitchen knives at the grocery store, the gas station, the hardware store, the sporting goods store, or the bait and tackle shop. Unless it is an emergency or you just need a knife to cut up bait, pass. The local big-box retailer is also not a place to buy good kitchen knives. Yes, they may actually have recognizable and reputable brand names, but not the top of their lines. The margins just aren't there. Stick with a specialty kitchenware shop, cutlery store, or online cutlery retailer. You *can* find decent knives in department stores, but the clerks don't have the knowledge or flexibility you need to get exactly what you want. You either buy their box or go home. Go home. You can do better.
- Price: Most of the time you do indeed get what you pay for. A good chef's knife generally costs somewhere between $80 and $150. Some are substantially more than that. There are some bargains out there and I'll point them out shortly, but for the most part a six-piece set of knives (with block!) for $49.95 is no bargain. Expect to pay upwards of $300—and more likely $400 to $500 and up—for a good matched set of knives, if that's how you are inclined.* This is a big reason I'm not a fan of boxed sets of knives. On a per-knife basis, a set can be a good deal but you also pay a hefty surcharge for knives you don't need. Most manufacturers offer a two- or three-piece "starter set" for this very reason.
- Mystery steel: If they won't tell you what's in the steel, they probably aren't very proud of it. There are also manufacturers who feel that you have no need for this information and would be too dumb to make use of it if you did. They don't deserve your business. On the other hand, some manufacturers etch their steel formula right onto the blades. Most have some description, if not the actual steel recipe, on the packaging. At a bare minimum, you should see the words "high carbon"

*There is one notable exception to the "you get what you pay for" rule, a bizarrely expensive line of knives sold only door to door. In that instance you most definitely do not get the quality you are paying for. Avoid them.

(Continued)

somewhere. That phrase is open to *very* flexible interpretation, but at least it means you are in the ballpark.

- Weasel words: Beware of meaningless marketingspeak, words like "surgical steel." There is no such thing. The word "stainless" all by itself without the high-carbon modifier tends to be a bad sign, too. It sounds authentic, but low-carbon stainless steel is awful. It is hard to sharpen and will not take or hold a decent working edge. It can be manufactured and sold cheaply, however, which is why a lot of people end up with knives that just make them miserable.

- Flex: Fillet knives aside, a good knife blade is fairly stiff. You shouldn't be able to bend it or flex it very much. If you can, that's usually a sign of cheap, low-carbon steel or a heat treatment that left the knife softer than you want in your kitchen. Hardness in knife blades is measured on the Rockwell C scale, so you'll sometimes see numbers like 58Rc, 58 Rockwell, or sometimes 58HRC. That means the hardness is 58 on the Rockwell scale. The absolute bare minimum you should accept is 56, though I consider that shamefully soft for a quality knife. My preference is for blades up around 60Rc, higher if I can get it. If the blade feels flimsy, it is.

- Never needs sharpening: Yes they do, you just don't want to. "Never needs sharpening" is the weasel term for a serrated edge, even if the maker tries strenuously to avoid calling it that. These knives are garbage. Avoid them at all costs. They are lousy performers to begin with and when they do eventually go dull they cannot easily be sharpened back to usefulness. They tend to be made with very cheap steel and depend entirely on the ripping action of the teeth to work. Might be handy in the tackle box, where corrosion resistance is more important than cutting ability, but these knives are not something worthy of your kitchen.

- Country of origin: The knife-making centers of the world are (or were) justly famous for their products: Solingen in Germany, Thiers in France, Sheffield in England, and Sakai and Seki City in Japan. When you buy a kitchen knife from one of these places, you stand a pretty good chance of getting a quality knife. When those manufacturers farm the work out to another country, you're probably getting cheap steel, punched out and slapped together by the thousands to feed the gaping maw of commerce. Put another way, a knife from Solingen stands a good chance of being high quality; a knife from a Solingen-based manufacturer that has the blades stamped out in Paraguay and assembled in Bora Bora probably isn't worth a damn, even if it does have the logo of a famous brand. ▲

Heart of Steel

I suspect that most folks don't give the steel in their knives a second thought. It's steel, right?

The fact is, there are hundreds of varieties of steel used for kitchen knives. Some are astounding. Some are worthless. Some will take a patina and look stained just like your grandmother's knives. Some wouldn't corrode if you left them in a bucket of battery acid.

Most popular kitchen knives fall into the category of "high-carbon stainless." These knives generally contain between .5 and .8 percent carbon, 13 to 18 percent chromium, and a little manganese, molybdenum, silicon, phosphorus, and sulfur. This makes for a steel that is easy to produce, is very stain resistant, and reasonably wear resistant. However, the quality—and the characteristics—of the steel a manufacturer uses is a major way to differentiate between various knife brands. Most of it is pretty good. Some is spectacular. Here's how to tell the difference.

An Overview of Steel

By definition, steel is a combination of iron and less than 2 percent carbon. For centuries, carbon was the only alloying element available. The problem in the early days of steel making was getting rid of unwanted elements, not adding new ones. However, modern kitchen knives are made with steel that includes a variety of nifty elements that are added to impart various characteristics. Manufacturers will frequently try to make their steel sound high tech and superior by throwing in terms you're not likely to know, but that sure sound cool. Here's the key to deciphering marketingspeak like "Advanced molybdenum vanadium steel Froz'n Forged® by Teutonic gnomes guarantees a razor sharp-edge."

Iron. This is the starting point. Iron alone is relatively soft.

It does not hold an edge well, wears quickly, and has little re-sistance to bending. Add a little bit of carbon and the story changes dramatically. The carbon combines with the iron to form hard carbide platelets cemented together in a matrix of iron. The combination is resistant to wear and bending and will take a keen edge.

Iron with just carbon as its primary alloy is called, oddly enough, "carbon steel."[*] This is the stuff your grandmother's knives were made from, the ones that were blotchy and dark gray. You can still buy carbon-steel knives. They stain and rust easily if not meticulously cared for, but they will take an amazing edge. A lot of serious knife nuts swear by carbon steel. Traditional Japanese knives are almost always carbon steel, and professional sushi chefs won't use anything else. Carbon steel can be made with a tighter grain structure than stainless steel. Smaller carbides and a tighter grain structure allow for a stronger, sharper edge. Other carbide formers, such as vanadium, can refine the grain of the steel further. Knives with a high vanadium content can take a very keen edge, but are harder to sharpen.

Carbon. Present in all steels, carbon is the most vital hard-ening element. The marketing folks will call anything with greater than .5 percent carbon content a "high-carbon" steel. But half a percent is hardly high by any definition. The cutoff that metallurgists use is called the "eutectoid point" and is just under .8 percent carbon. Anything above that can legitimately be called a high-carbon steel. As a rule of thumb, the higher the carbon content, the harder the steel will be and the better it will perform in the kitchen. My favorite kitchen steel, VG10, is around 1.05 percent carbon. There is a trade-off. Higher carbon content can make stainless knives, well, less

*Again, for the metallurgists in the audience, yes there will always be a little bit of manganese and minute amounts of sulfur and phosphorus.

stainless. High-performance knives tend to be less corrosion-resistant than standard kitchen knives. That's a compromise well worth making.

Chromium. Added for corrosion resistance. A steel with a little more than 12 percent chromium is considered stainless, though all knife blades will stain or rust if not cared for properly. Stainless knives are just a little more forgiving of neglect. Chromium is a carbide former, so it also increases wear resistance.

Cobalt. Increases strength and hardness and refines the grain structure of the steel. Allows the steel to be quenched at higher temperatures and intensifies the effects of other alloys. Cobalt is generally only found in VG10 or ATS55. Both are excellent steels, so if the description has cobalt listed as an ingredient, you're probably in pretty good shape.

Manganese. Aids grain structure, increases hardenability and wear resistance. Manganese is present in most cutlery steels because it makes the steel more responsive to heat treatment.

Molybdenum. Another carbide former. Increases hardness, prevents brittleness, makes the steel easier to machine. The addition of molybdenum, usually just called moly, helps chromium do its job better.

Nickel. Adds toughness and possibly aids in corrosion resistance. Nickel is generally used in the type of stainless steel that they make pots, pans, and sinks out of, rather than high-quality kitchen knives. Nickel in a knife steel is usually a sign of cafeteria-grade cutlery.

Phosphorus. Essentially a contaminant.

Silicon. Increases hardness and strength.

Sulfur. Increases machinability but decreases toughness.

Tungsten. Increases heat, wear, and shock resistance. Tungsten is the strongest carbide former behind vanadium.

Vanadium. Another carbide former. Contributes to wear resistance and hardenability. Vanadium refines the grain of the steel, which contributes to toughness and allows the blade to take a very sharp edge.

Let's put our newfound knowledge to use. Wüsthof makes some of the best-selling kitchen knives around, and for good reason. They kindly stamp the blades with their steel formula so you know what you're getting. When you see X50CrMoV15, you can decipher it as approximately .5 percent carbon (X for some reason, I don't know why they don't use C) with the 15 made up of chromium, molybdenum, and vanadium—most likely 14 to 14.5 percent chromium, .5 to .8 molybdenum, and .1 to .2 vanadium (a little goes a long way). That gives you a knife blade that will be extremely corrosion resistant and that will take and hold a decent edge. However, the moderate carbon content means that the steel might be a little soft. A quick check of Wüsthof's marketing materials shows that they temper the steel to 56Rc, which is the absolute bare minimum you should accept in the kitchen.

Chef's Choice also makes very fine kitchen knives. Their formula is something along the lines of 1 percent carbon, 14 percent chromium, and 3 to 4 percent molybdenum. The higher carbon content tells you that the steel is most likely going to be harder than the previous example. Sure enough, Chef's Choice tempers their knives to 60Rc. The potential loss of stain resistance is counterbalanced with a higher molybdenum content.

Many manufacturers are a little cagey about *exactly* what goes into their steel (as though their competitors can't take a blade down to the lab and figure it out in a matter of minutes). They do sometimes give you clues. If you see molybdenum and vanadium in the blurb on the box, you're probably dealing with something along the lines of the Wüsthof formula. Decent stuff. If you see tungsten listed, the steel will be very wear resistant and hold an edge for a very long time. If you see cobalt, you're probably dealing with VG10, an excellent kitchen steel. If the manufacturer specifies Swedish steel, you probably have something along the lines of AEBL or 12C27.

If the manufacturer deigns to give you more specific information, some of the steel types you might find in a kitchen knife include:

- 420J (American)
- 425M (American)
- 440A, B, and C (American)
- 1.4116 (German)
- MBS26 (Japanese)
- VG10 (Japanese)
- AEBL (Swedish)
- 12C27 (Swedish)

They are all decent performers. Some are much better than others, though. I wouldn't make garbage can lids out of 420J or 440A, but some manufacturers do use them for kitchen knives. If you own or lust after a knife made in Solingen, Germany, you will very likely end up with 1.4116 or a variation on it. You will sometimes see 1.4116 spelled out as X50CrMoV15. It is pretty darned good stuff, remember? It is stain resistant and tough and will take a decent edge, but usually falls down in the hardness department. The German manufacturers tend to leave it a little soft at 54 to 56 on the Rockwell scale. I've even seen some knives as low as 52Rc. That's pathetic. The argument goes that softer steel will roll or dent rather than chip if it is abused, and it's easier to keep sharp. The truth is that the softer steel won't hold an edge for very long, so it requires more maintenance. Because the edge of the soft steel is prone to rolling, the manufacturers put very thick edges on their knives, further decreasing performance to blunt-object levels. The problem is that fixing the situation by upping the carbon levels or bumping up the Rockwell hardness decreases corrosion resistance and toughness. The blades become less stainless and more brittle.

In addition to their homegrown steels, Japanese manufacturers frequently use Swedish steels like AEBL, 12C27, and its big brother 19C27 for stainless knives. One of the most common Japanese wonder steels on the market is VG10. It is generally hardened to 60Rc or so and takes and holds an edge that even at high polish levels feels aggressive and toothy. Solid VG10 often takes a light patina almost like carbon steel, so manufacturers tend to clad it with softer, sometimes decorative, stainless steel, leaving just the cutting edge of VG10 exposed. This is actually a clever solution. Not only do you get the nicer-looking, easier-to-care-for steel on the outside and the high-performance steel for the edge, it also allows the manufacturer to cushion the possibly brittle core with something with a little more flex and give. It's an ancient sword- and axe-making technique that has found new life in the modern kitchen. Many Japanese knives are constructed in a similar fashion, with a very hard, generally nonstainless core laminated with a softer steel for added toughness.

Note the characteristic wavy lines of the *suminigashi*-patterned softer outer steel, which is forge-welded to a core of harder steel that forms the edge. The pattern is purely decorative and not all knives made this way have it.

If you get into Japanese knives there are two other steels you will quickly become acquainted with: *shiro-ko* and *ao-ko*, or "white steel" and "blue steel." They are also sometimes called *shirogami* ("white paper") and *aogami* ("blue paper") after the color of the labels Hitachi, the steel manufacturer, puts on them. Shiro-ko is a very pure low-alloy straight carbon steel that will take an amazingly sharp edge. Ao-ko has a little chromium and tungsten added for extra wear resistance. In theory, ao-ko will not get as sharp as shiro-ko but will hold its edge longer. In practice, you'll never be able to tell the difference. Neither steel is stainless. Most traditional Japanese knives are not.

If you have a custom knife made, your choices open up considerably. There are some astonishing steels out there (like S30V and CPM154) but most of them are not cost effective for mass-produced knives.

Sharp as a . . .

Knife performance is all about steel and geometry. After working through the sharpening section of the book, you will be able to put an edge on your knives that would make the manufacturer hang his head in shame. At the very least, you'll know what to ask for when you visit a professional knife sharpener.

To a lot of people, though, a knife's sharpness right out of the box is about the best it will ever be. That's too bad. Once you get the hang of sharpening your own knives, you'll sneer at factory edges forevermore.★ Factory edges cut reasonably well for a little while, but they are much thicker than they need to be and are a lot sloppier than you would ever imagine. I spent a couple of afternoons peering through a high-powered microscope at the out-of-the-box edges of a gaggle of top-dollar chef's knives. It was appalling.

★I'm Southern, so I do a little one-lip curl, Elvis sort of sneer, but you can sneer any way you like.

CARBON STEEL VERSUS STAINLESS STEEL

The great debate rages on. Advocates of straight carbon (nonstainless) steel claim that their knives take a keener edge, hold it longer, and are easier to resharpen than stainless-steel knives. Stainless-steel users claim that carbon-steel knives are unsanitary and leave an off-taste in foods, and that stainless knives hold an edge longer than their carbon counterparts.

Who's right? Depends on your definitions and your environment. It's not as simple as carbon versus stainless.

Carbon steels range from simple iron-carbon combinations to high-alloy tool steels that will cut through concrete without losing their edge. Stainless steels vary from very soft, extremely stain-resistant scuba diving knives to super stainless alloys, like Crucible Materials's S30V, a steel tailor-made for the custom cutlery industry.

For use in the kitchen, the carbon steel devotees are right. Modern carbon-steel kitchen knives generally *are* a little harder and stronger than stainless-steel kitchen knives. They are easy to sharpen and take a screaming edge. And while the patina that develops on a carbon knife can be unsightly (unless you like that sort of thing), it isn't unsanitary. These knives can impart a distinctive taste to acidic foods until the patina is fully built up. Carbon steel is finer grained and makes for a knife that can be tweaked to astounding performance levels. Professional sushi chefs rarely use anything else.

There is a catch, though. (You knew there had to be.)

Carbon-steel knives are fussy and demand more attention than a purebred Chihuahua. Unless you are absolutely meticulous in your care, they will rapidly lose their performance advantages.

For the average user, modern high-carbon stainless steel rules in the wet, acidic conditions of the kitchen. For all their faults, compromises, and shortcomings, stainless-steel kitchen knives work better and will hold their edges longer than carbon-steel knives.

The culprit is corrosion—the effects of acid and microrusting. Even on what appears to be a mirror-bright, razor-sharp edge, microscopic particles of rust and corrosion will form, attacking the edge and reducing its performance. Unless carbon-steel knives are rinsed and dried immediately after each use, their edges will degrade quickly in kitchen use. The stainless edge will easily outlast them.

An opposing view: "Take care of your things. Slow down. Pay attention. Carbon steel doesn't take that much more work and it takes an incredibly keen edge. Appreciate what it can do. You would rinse and dry stainless knives anyway," says ABS Master Bladesmith Bob Kramer, whose carbon-steel kitchen knives are regarded as some of the finest knives available. ▲

However, that factory edge is how the vast majority of people will judge the performance of their knives. Who can blame them? You buy a knife, you expect it to be sharp. The edge bevels look clean and even and haven't been boogered up by your father-in-law's ham-handed sharpening efforts prior to the annual Thanksgiving feast and family-recrimination session. Your kids haven't run them through the grinder on the back of the can opener to see the pretty sparks. They're new. It's like starting over.

You know what? There's a lot of appeal to that. So let's make sure you get out of the store with knives that are going to keep the fantasy alive—at least for a month or two. Then we'll tune those babies up so that you'll be begging your family to put up with onion soup *again* just so you can dice a couple more.

Stand under a strong light—sunlight is best, if the store will let you take your chosen knife outside. Hold the knife out in front of you with the spine facing down and the edge up so that your light source hits it squarely and you can see the whole length of the edge. You are looking for the telltale glint of a rolled edge. A cleanly formed sharp edge will not reflect light. Move the blade around a little under the light. You should see the sides of the knife forming a thicker and thicker V toward the spine, but you should not see the edge itself. If you do, or if you see little hotspots of light, you have an edge that has rolled over to one side a little. It won't be sharp in those areas. See more than a couple of those glints? Hand the knife back to the counter guy and ask for another one. While you are at it, check to ensure that the blade is nice and straight and that the tip isn't bent. If you are buying a set, check every knife in it. Yes, every one. It just takes a minute or two. Yes, it will probably annoy the clerk. You wouldn't take home a new car with bald tires, would you? This is the most basic quality control test there is. If each knife doesn't pass, swap it out for one that does. There is no reason to put up with sloppy edges or bent tips on your new knives.

Next up on the quality edge checklist: take a look at the scratch pattern on the edge bevel—the bevel is the little V at the very edge of the knife where the flat sides of the blade take a sudden turn toward the center. Sometimes the scratch pattern can be a little hard to see, especially if you normally wear reading glasses for anything smaller than the headlines in the newspaper. If you see a lot of coarse grooves, move on. In general, the smoother and more polished the edge, the better it's going to perform in the kitchen. You sometimes read or hear about "toothy" edges. There is a time and a place for a toothy edge. This ain't it. Those teeth should be nearly microscopic. If you can see them with the naked eye, they're too big.

Sometimes you can be fooled. I have a knife whose edge looked like it had been ground with a cinderblock when I first purchased it, but it cut like a scalpel. I couldn't figure it out until I used a photographer's loupe to examine the edge. There was *another* bevel on top of the first, a hair-thin, highly polished microbevel at the very apex of edge. I've been putting compound bevels on my knives for years, but this was the first time I'd seen a manufacturer do it. Very smart. And fairly easy to spot if you know what you're looking for. If you are examining the scratch pattern of a knife, start with the knife flat and horizontal. Slowly rotate the edge upward until the coarse scratches disappear into the side of the knife. If there is still a bright, shiny strip at the very edge of the edge, you might have a double bevel. Check the other side to be sure. It should match.

Sometimes, despite your best efforts, you get a knife home that just doesn't perform. It might pass the glint test and have a reasonably polished edge. It might even shave hair or slice newsprint (two of the standard tests for sharpness; we'll cover them on page 184 in "How to Tell If Your Knife Is Sharp"), but feels more like a first-grader's pencil when it's going through a potato. It could be that you have a very slightly rolled edge, too small to see. A couple of quick strokes down your fine-grit ceramic rod should fix it right up. You did get a ceramic rod, didn't you? If not, go back and get one.

Here's the problem: many knives are sharpened on high-speed grinding wheels or belt sanders that leave a very light burr (more on burrs in the sharpening section) or rolled edge. The edge may be sharp, it's just not pointing straight up and down. It's been pushed over to the side a little. If the edge will shave on one side of the blade but not the other, that's your clue that you've got a rolled edge. The ceramic rod or fine-grooved steel—used with a very light touch—will push everything back into alignment. Voilà. Goodbye first-grade pencil, hello lightsaber.

NOW YOU KNOW

There you have it, probably more than you wanted to know about what to look for when you're ready to buy your knives. It's certainly more than the average clerk at the knife counter knows. If he (and, yes, I mean he—it's always the male clerks who think they are knife gods) gives you any guff, hit him with the heat treating info or your newfound metallurgy prowess and watch him go slack jawed. Throw in "eutectoid point" if you want to be really cruel.

Now you know that when you are buying high-quality cutlery, the old advice about full-tang, full-bolster forged knives goes right out the window. You know that forged knives *are* pretty darn good for the most part, but modern machined knives are, too. It comes down to a matter of feel. Do you like heavy knives? Go for the forged model. Favor something thinner and lighter? Machined, all the way. There are even some knives that strike a nice balance between the two styles. The most important factor is how the knife feels in your hands (and on your wallet).

You can decipher the marketing doublespeak about advanced chrome-molybdenum this and vanadium carbide that.

More important, you know how to stay away from the cheap, nasty stuff. You also know that a big ol' block of knives isn't always the bargain it seems.

So grab your credit card, birthday money, large inheritance check, or carefully hoarded cash from your summer job and let's go shopping. We can outfit your kitchen with high-performance knives on any budget.

2

TYPES OF KNIVES AND THEIR USES

When you are ready to outfit your kitchen, you really only need three knives, tops. You can get away with two if you are a purist or funds are limited. As for how many knives you might eventually end up with? The sky is the limit. There is a knife for just about everything under the sun, from stubby oyster knives to giant tuna swords. The Holy Trinity of the kitchen, though, is the chef's knife, the paring knife, and the slicing knife or bread knife. Your chef's knife and paring knife will see the most action, so the third knife is really your *option knife*. If you eat a lot of fish, you might want a fillet knife or flexible boning knife rather than a bread knife. If you are a veggie fan or are into Asian cooking, a vegetable cleaver might be more up your alley. Let's start with the biggies, then we can mix and match to meet any budget or cooking style.

There are only two really important decisions in a cook's life: choosing a mate and buying a chef's knife. If that seems like an overstatement, you just haven't found the right knife.

—RUSS PARSONS, *LA Times* food columnist and author of *How to Pick a Peach*

Two traditional single-beveled Japanese knives: *usuba* (left) and *yanagiba* (right).

THREE FAMILIES OF KNIVES

The kitchen knives available to most of the United States come in three distinct families: traditional Western knives, traditional Japanese knives, and Japanese-made Western-style knives.

The vast majority of knives in the United States today are *traditional Western or European knives.* These may be German, French, American, or nowadays even made in China, but they are the historically European knives we all know and love—the classic chef's knife, paring knife, boning knife, bread knife, et al. found in every major department store and kitchenware store. They are made by Wüsthof, Henckels, Sabatier, Chef's Choice, Messermeister, Forschner/Victorinox, Lamson, and dozens of other manufacturers.

Then there are the *traditional Japanese knives.* You rarely see these outside of Asian markets, specialty retailers, or sushi bars. They have thick spines with a wide single bevel on the front side. The back side of the knife is basically flat. They are generally manufactured in a laborious hand-forging process by small families of knife makers. They usually are made from straight carbon steel and are not stainless at all. They often have oval or octagonal wooden handles. The long, narrow sushi knife is called a *yanagiba,* or "willow leaf blade." There is a vegetable knife called either an *usuba* or *nakiri* depending on the shape of the blade. The third primary member of the traditional Japanese knife family is the *deba,* which is used for heavy chopping. These knives are task specific and are not particularly well suited to non-Japanese cooking. The single-sided edge bevel means they have a very acute edge angle and can be astoundingly sharp.

Somewhere in the middle is a third category that is rapidly gaining prominence: *Japanese-made Western-style knives.* They come in familiar shapes but are made from thinner, harder steel and are lighter than their traditional Western counterparts. For the most part they are machined rather than forged. While they are outstanding performers, Japanese-made Western-style knives sometimes can be a little lacking in the fit and finish department. Even on the expensive models the handle slabs, tang, and rivets aren't always as smooth as they are on pricey European knives. Just something to pay attention to. The chef's knife is called a *gyuto* and looks pretty much like a French chef's knife. The other knives to note are the *sujihiki*, which is exactly like the long slicing knives we are used to; the *petty* (from the French *petit* or small), which is slightly longer and narrower than a paring knife; the all-purpose *santoku*; and the *honesuki*, which is technically a poultry boning knife but in a Western kitchen makes for a great small utility knife. Global, Shun, and MAC are three of the better-known makers of Western-style Japanese knives but there are dozens more worth seeking out, too.

There are plenty of other knife styles and knife traditions from around the world, including the truly wonderful Chinese cleaver, but these are the three basic families of knives you'll find when you go knife shopping. ▲

The Japanese chef treats his knives as if they were sacred objects, not just tools. Japanese chefs handle their knives with reverence, not to mention with great care.

—MASAHARU MORIMOTO, Iron Chef and owner of
Morimoto restaurant

THE BIG ONE: THE CHEF'S KNIFE

The chef's knife is the first knife you pick up in the kitchen and the last one you put down. You can do 90 percent of everything you ever need to do in the kitchen with just a chef's knife. You can do 100 percent if you really have to. This is the Big Kahuna. If you have $150 to spend on knives, at least $100 of it should go toward the chef's knife, probably more. It is not just the most important knife in your kitchen; it is the most important *tool* in your kitchen. Buy accordingly. Even if you are brand new to cooking, very soon you won't be able to imagine trying to prepare a meal without your chef's knife. It is your paintbrush, your means of self-expression—and more important, your means of getting dinner on the table. Expect to pay somewhere between $85 to $150 for a good one. Some chef's knives go for more than $250 for a standard 8-inch knife, but there are bargains out there, too.

Chef's knives (referred to by old-school chefs as "French knives") range from 6 inches to 12 inches or more, the most common lengths being 8 inches and 10 inches. Blades under 8 inches are too short to reach all the way across a pot roast and will lead to nothing but frustration. Part of the reason I like Japanese-made Western-style knives so much is that they come in handy in-between sizes. Gyutos, the Japanese equivalent to our chef's knives, come in 210 mm (about 8.25 inches), 240 mm (about 9.5 inches), 270 mm (a little over 10.5 inches), and 300 mm (just under 12 inches). Yes, you do have to use the metric system.

Why Western knives make such a huge jump from 8 to 10 inches is beyond me. One German manufacturer, Messermeister, does make a 9-inch chef's knife, and it is just about perfect. The 240 mm and 270 mm lengths also strike a nice balance between heft, length, and manageability (which also includes the "don't freak out the spouse or guest" factor). You need the length, but with the length comes width. And width is a very good thing. A wide blade allows you to conveniently scoop up your neatly diced ingredients so you can toss them in a pan. One minor drawback is that a smaller knife block may not accommodate a knife that is wider than 2 inches at the heel. Don't forget, though, a chef's knife is about more than the edge. That wide blade that makes for such a great scoop? It also excels at smashing garlic. The spine of the knife can be used for cracking crabs. When you are doing precision cuts like a julienne, the spine of the knife also makes for a great ruler to judge the thickness of your slices.

I'm suspicious of anyone who doesn't use a broad-bladed chef's knife.

—MICHAEL RUHLMAN, author of *The Elements of Cooking*

The relatively thick spine tapers down to a thin edge, but it also narrows toward the tip (called "distal taper" if you want to toss some cool knifespeak into the conversation). That makes for a very fine tip that is perfect for precision work like mincing shallots. With practice, you bone a chicken or core strawberries almost as easily with your chef's knife as with the smaller boning knives or paring knives.

The majority of the action occurs along the cutting edge. Here you have another choice to make. There are now three distinct blade profiles to choose from. The dominant German-style knives have more "belly." They curve a bit starting from about three-quarters of the way up the blade (from the heel) to the tip, creating a rounded area that is great for that rocking motion used when slicing. The area below the belly is relatively straight. French-pattern knives tend to have a straighter line between heel and tip, making a more uniform triangle with less belly. This blade shape is especially well suited for the fussy cuts of classical French cuisine. The Japanese gyuto is somewhere in between, though it is slightly closer to the French style. The length of the edge means that you are distributing the cutting job over a greater area, reducing the effort needed. You can do everything from portioning steaks to cutting basil into chiffonade with the long, sharp cutting edge of your chef's knife.

Note the blade shapes of these three chef's knives. The top has a German-style curved belly, the second is the flatter French profile, and the third is the Japanese gyuto style.

The heel of the blade (well, actually the area 2 to 3 inches forward of the heel on back to the heel itself) is for heavy-duty work. The blade is at its thickest and widest here so you can concentrate a lot of force into a very small area without risk of damaging your knife. This is one area where German- and French-patterned knives have a slight advantage over Japanese gyutos. The thicker, heavier bolstered knives are better at chopping through light bones than the thinner, lighter gyutos. Each style of knife can handle tough vegetables like butternut squash with ease, but if you are in the habit of hacking through bone, a heavy bolstered knife in the French or German style might suit your cooking style better.

> I discovered I didn't have to "keep up with the boys." A 10-inch knife put me on equal footing with the men in the kitchen. It gave me the same power.
>
> —SARA MOULTON, Executive Chef, *Gourmet* magazine, author of *Sara's Secrets for Weeknight Meals*

THREE VIRTUES AND A COW SWORD: THE SANTOKU AND GYUTO

If you have been upright and breathing over the last couple of years, you've probably already seen or heard of the santoku, the thin, wide-bladed Japanese utility knife that, due to clever marketing and perky celebrity endorsements, has taken the cooking world by storm. Even people who would never have otherwise set foot in a Towels'n'Such or Gourmet Hut are wandering in looking to purchase a santoku. That's wonderful. Anything that spreads the gospel of good kitchen knives is fine by me.

Three variations on the santoku or "knife of three virtues."

Santoku translates as "knife of three virtues." Unfortunately, no one can actually tell you exactly what those three virtues are. One explanation says the three virtues are the tip of the knife for fine work, the cutting edge for general duty, and the heel of the knife for heavy-duty chopping. Another theory suggests that the three virtues are excellence in slicing, mincing, and chopping. And yet a third explanation takes the view that the three virtues involve the ability to adroitly handle fish, vegetables, and meats. It's nine virtues for the price of three! What a bargain.

The third theory seems most credible. Japanese knives can be very task specific. In most households there is a knife for fish, a knife for vegetables, and a cruiserweight brute of a knife called a *deba* that is used for liberating a fish's head from its body and other grisly chores that involve hacking through bones.

The santoku can't manage any of these tasks with the same aplomb as the dedicated knife. You won't find many sushi masters trading in their pampered yanagibas for a down-home santoku anytime soon. But the santoku does do a lot of things reasonably well and makes for a pretty nifty do-all kitchen tool.

I find them a little short for use as a primary kitchen knife for the same reason that I don't like chef's knives under 8 inches. You can't slice a turkey, for example, but a santoku is great for making short work of family portions of veggies—and the wide blade is great for scooping. If you do decide to get virtuous, go for a blade length of at least 6.5 to 7 inches. Anything less than that just isn't effective and will lead to frustration. The blade of a santoku is less curved (has less belly) than the chef's knives you might be used to. The santoku is meant to be used in a forward-and-down kind of slice rather than a rocking motion. The technique is just as fast as the rocking motion and can be more precise, but it does take a little getting used to. Santokus with more belly act more like a traditional chef's knife. Either way, if you eat a lot of vegetables or don't cook large cuts of meat, you can get away with just a santoku and be pretty happy in the kitchen. If you do prepare roasts or cook larger vegetables such as butternut squash or pumpkin, the santoku is better suited to playing backup to a larger chef's knife. In this role it shines, so I suppose it doesn't really matter how many virtues it has.

It's really too bad you can't take Japanese knife names too literally because my favorite knife, the gyuto, translates directly to "cow sword." I love the idea of owning a cow sword.

It makes me giggle maniacally just thinking about it. More prosaically, the gyuto is usually translated as "large meat knife" and up until fairly recently wasn't discussed in polite company. These things are amazing. The gyuto takes the shape of a classic French chef's knife, hot rods the profile, and matches it with some of the best steel on the planet. You need a cow sword.

Two gyutos, one with a custom-made Japanese-style handle (a *wa-gyuto*) and one with a standard European-style handle.

Gyutos have an almost cultlike following among professional chefs and kitchen knife cognoscenti. While many pros still cling to their heavy iron from Solingen, others are abandoning their traditional knives (and repetitive stress injuries) and becoming evangelical converts once they get their hands on a gyuto. Remember our earlier discussion about modern machined knives? This is them. They are not drop forged like German and French chef's knives. Like most Japanese-made Western-style knives, they are cut (often with lasers) from thin bars of high-tech steel and ground to shape. They are much thinner than forged knives and have less belly than the traditional German shape. In fact, they closely resemble the classic triangular French shape that was in vogue before the German knives became the dominant market force and kitchen fashion. Even better, gyutos sport Western-style handles, so they feel just like a trim, buff, hardbody version of the knives you are already familiar with.

Gyutos usually come with much more acute edge angles than their European or American counterparts—15 degrees per side as opposed to 22 to 26 degrees per side for the more traditional knives. They also come with much harder steel, 59 to 61Rc is pretty common, unlike the softer 52 to 56Rc of the stuff you're used to seeing. That makes for a screaming sharp edge that will last for an astonishingly long time. On the downside, that also means that the edge will be somewhat more delicate than the softer, tougher Western edge. You can't bang these knives on the countertop or whack through heavy bone. If you are really hard on your knives or work in a kitchen where someone is apt to grab your knife to use as an impromptu can opener, you are probably better off trading high performance for greater durability. You also have my permission to take the offending doofus out back and perform an attitude adjustment, preferably with some sort of blunt object.

One of the nicest things about the thinner, lighter gyuto is that you can use more knife for the same weight penalty. For example, an 8-inch European-style chef's knife weighs about ten ounces. A comparable gyuto weighs between 6 and 6½ ounces. A 10-inch gyuto might weigh a little more than 9 ounces. So you can trade up from an 8-inch chef's knife to a 10-inch gyuto and get more reach and cutting ability. Or you could go up a little in length to 240mm (a standard size for gyutos, about 9.5 inches), get more reach, *and* reduce the weight hanging off the end of your wrists. That makes a huge difference when you are standing at a cutting board for hours at a time. You might not have to dice 5 pounds of carrots or 10 pounds of butternut squash every day as a busy prep cook would, but even dicing a soup pot full of potatoes for a large family or church supper will take a toll on your wrists. Many culinary schools teach that a heavy knife will do some of the work for you. That's true, but superior geometry will do the same. A thinner, sharper knife will outperform a heavier, more wedge-shaped knife with less effort on your part. If you have only used thick-bladed European-style knives, the thin blade of a santoku or gyuto will be a revelation. It all depends on your comfort level with each style, your technique, and your environment. Even if you are a hard-core traditionalist, you owe it to yourself to test-drive a gyuto. You just might be impressed.

THE LITTLE ONES: PARING KNIVES

The next player in the kitchen triumvirate is the paring knife. This is the microsurgery version of the chef's knife. Paring knives are used for all those delicate little tasks—scoring orange peels, cutting the cores out of apple quarters, removing eyes from potatoes, hulling strawberries. The paring knife is perfect for those chores where a chef's knife would be unwieldy. The blade usually ranges from 2 inches to about 4 inches in length and comes in a variety of shapes. Some taper to a point like a chef's knife. Others have a straight edge and a spine that curves radically down to meet it at the very end. This is called a sheepsfoot blade and it works kind of like a miniature santoku. Unlike the santoku, however, there is no knuckle clearance, so you can't effectively use the full length of the blade on the cutting board. If you tend to hold a carrot up in one hand and cut against your thumb with the other (the grandmother technique), a sheepsfoot paring knife gives you a lot of edge for its size. If you use your paring knife on a cutting board or use the "pointer technique" where you lay your index finger along the spine of the blade, a standard paring knife is probably a better fit.

From top to bottom: bird's beak (tourné) knife, sheepsfoot paring knife, spearpoint paring knife, petty (petit) knife.

Then there is the tourné knife or bird's beak parer. It has a curved blade that is used for the dreaded tourné cut, a classic French vegetable cut that transforms a two-inch chunk of root vegetable into a seven-sided football. *Tourner* is French for "to turn." Though seldom seen outside the rarefied atmosphere of very expensive, very old-school restaurants, the tourné cut is considered pretty swanky and is sometimes used as an indicator of a professional cook's knife skills. The curved blade does come in handy when peeling round surfaces. If you don't work in a professional kitchen, though, skip it. A standard peeler does a better job.

> **When buying or recommending knives for others, find out what kind of cook they are rather than what kind of cook they want to be. Buy them the knife they need *now*, not what they might need five years from now.**
>
> —RUSS PARSONS, *LA Times* food columnist and author of *How to Pick a Peach*

SLICE OF LIFE: SLICERS AND BREAD KNIVES

The greyhounds of the kitchen, slicers are long and lean. Slicers start at 9 inches and are available up to 18 inches. The length of the blade allows you to make a clean slice in a single stroke. This is especially important when carving roasted meats or slicing fish. Excessive sawing back and forth leaves ridges and a rough texture that is unattractive. The narrowness of the blade help keep moist foods from sticking. Some slicers, especially those intended for catering use, have rounded tips that not only help the cook keep from tearing a beautiful salmon but also keep him from spearing the guests as they go through the buffet line.

Slicers and carving knives come with a variety of edges. Meat and fish slicers often have a *Granton edge*, a series of ovals hollowed into the blade that create air pockets between the blade and the delicate flesh to keep it from sticking and shredding. This actually works on narrow slicing blades. Attempts to transplant the idea to chef's knives and santokus have been less successful. The ovals (called *kullens* or a *kullenschliff* edge) don't take up enough surface area on a wider blade to make much difference, though one knife manufacturer, Glestain, has taken the idea to the extreme, dimpling their knives with rows of huge pockets. It looks weird but actually works pretty darn well.

From top to bottom: a scalloped combination bread knife/slicer, a deeply dimpled Glestain slicing knife, a plain edge slicer, and a Granton edge slicer.

Bread knives usually have *serrated edges*, a series of saw teeth ground into the edge separated by crescents of sharpened edge. The teeth provide an aggressive bite that keeps the knife from slipping on a hard crust, but the crescents do the actual slicing. In part, the teeth are there to protect the insides of the serrations. Serrated knives don't need to be made from especially good steel or have an especially keen edge. The serrations do all the work. At least for a little while. Then the teeth wear down or roll over and the insides of the serrations start to dull, too. There are techniques for sharpening serrated knives, but it is a pain. Don't bother. For the most part you can treat bread knives as disposable items. Head down to your local restaurant supply store and pick up whatever commercial brand is on sale. You need a bread knife between 10 and 12 inches long. Any shorter and you won't be able to slice through a boule or crusty artisanal loaf without a lot of sawing and cursing. Any longer and you'll have storage problems. Use it for a couple of years, and when it is no longer sharp buy a new one. That is part of the reason I don't like the bread knives that come with most knife blocks. They are too short and too expensive for their task. Serrated knives are not delicate tools and certainly don't need to cost as much as your chef's knife. They are the plastic ballpoint pens of the knife world, cheap and interchangeable. Just don't expect too much from them and you'll be happy.

Scalloped edge, Granton edge, and serrated edge.

If that offends your sensibilities, you can get a 10-inch slicer with a *scalloped edge*. Scallops are the exact opposite of serrations. Instead of the little crescents being on the inside, protected by triangular teeth, the pattern is reversed. The scalloped crescents *are* the cutting edge, separated by little triangular indentations. A scalloped-edge slicer can do double duty as a good slicing knife and a good bread knife. Scalloped edges are more gentle than serrated edges and generally leave a cleaner cut. My two favorite bread knives, the MAC SB015 and the Wüsthof Super Slicer, both have scalloped edges. They are excellent bread knives and double as competent meat slicers.

That's it for the Big Three. You can do anything and everything you ever need to do in a home kitchen with a good chef's knife, a paring knife, and a slicer or bread knife. However, there are some great knives out there that are a little more specialized and make some tasks easier.

CLOSE TO THE BONE: BONING AND FILLET KNIVES

Boning knives and fillet knives have a lot in common. They are generally 6 to 8 inches long, though specialty fillet knives can get much longer. Both have thin, narrow blades that curve upward to the tip. The difference is the flex. Boning knives tend to be rigid while some fillet knives can bend nearly in half. The flex of the fillet knife allows you to gently bow the knife into position and, if you're doing it right, glide the flesh right off the fish's bones, leaving little behind. The rigidity of a boning knife is handy when you are boning a leg of lamb, trimming silverskin from a tenderloin, or removing the fat cap from a brisket.

Where things get confusing is that there are flexible boning knives and stiff fillet knives. If you are buying knives one at a time, consider which you do more, fillet fish or bone and trim meats, and purchase accordingly. You can also split the difference and get a semiflexible boning knife and be done with it.

A fillet knife is significantly more flexible than a boning knife.

One thing to look for with either type of knife is a lip that curves downward at the front of the handle just in front of your fingers. A fillet or boning knife has a blade narrower than the handle. Without that lip or bolster there is the risk of stubbing. That's the butcher's term for hitting something (usually a bone) with the tip of the knife hard enough to cause your hand to slide up onto the blade. This can be extremely painful and messy. Cheap fillet knives, like those sold at bait shops and sporting goods stores, are notorious for this. You need that lip.

A honesuki (Japanese poultry boning knife) and standard Western-style boning knife.

To make matters just a little more confusing, there is also the honesuki, the Japanese poultry boning knife. Honesukis have wider, sharply triangular blades and pointed tips. Some are ground only on one side and are flat on the back. Others are ground on both sides like traditional Western knives, but the bevel may be asymmetrical. As you might expect from a somewhat specialized knife, the honesuki excels at deboning chicken. The tip works along the bones just like a Western boning knife. The thicker heel makes going through joints or ribcage a breeze. And unlike Western boning and fillet knives, the honesuki actually has enough clearance to slice straight down on a cutting board without banging your knuckles, which means it can double as a general-purpose utility knife. However, the strengths that make the honesuki such a whiz with chicken are its liabilities when dealing with larger cuts of beef, pork, or lamb. The wider, thicker blade is harder to work into small areas and tends to cleave the meat more than a regular boning knife. If you eat a lot of chicken, though, this knife is hard to beat.

"UTILITY" KNIVES

Smaller than a chef's knife, larger than a paring knife, the so-called utility knife is usually 5 to 7 inches long and fairly narrow. They are not really good for much. They are too long to be used for peeling and too small for any significant slicing. They sometimes come with a serrated blade and are called sandwich or tomato knives. In those roles, the utility knife does a respectable job, but slicing the occasional sandwich or tomato doesn't justify the price tag. This is the type of knife used as filler in most block sets. You pay for it, but you'll rarely use it.

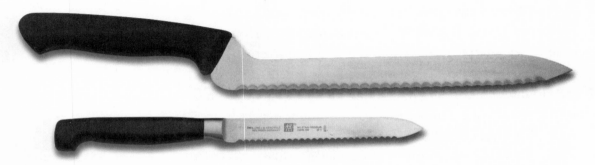

The Z-shaped deli knife is generally more useful than a utility or tomato knife.

Part of the problem is that the length and narrowness of the knife really only allows you to use about half the blade on the cutting board. You have to cut at an angle with the back half of the knife lifted enough to keep your hand off the board. In that position, a 7-inch utility knife has about 4 inches of usable length. A better alternative is the offset bread knife, also called a deli knife. The Z shape puts your hand higher than the blade so you can use the entire length. The offset deli knife, especially the serrated version, makes short work of sandwiches, tomatoes, cucumbers, baguettes, hoagie rolls, heads of lettuce, or just about any situation where you need a medium-sized knife. In fact, because you can use the entire length of the blade, you could get away with using an 8-inch (or longer) one as your bread knife, too. This knife actually does have some utility and makes a great addition to the knife block.

HELLO MR. CLEAVER: CHINESE CLEAVERS AND VEGETABLE KNIVES

Very few people need a heavy bone cleaver these days. We rarely buy sides of beef or bone-in primal cuts of meat. Basic chopping can be handled with aplomb by nearly any chef's knife on the market. So why mention cleavers at all? Because while the heavy meat cleaver is very much a specialty item, the thin-bladed Chinese cleaver is a do-all kitchen wonder.

Be adventurous! Once you use a Chinese cleaver, you'll realize how wonderful it is. Have the courage to try something new.

—MARTIN YAN, cookbook author and host of *Yan Can Cook*

The Chinese cleaver rivals the chef's knife as an all-purpose tool, and in a one-knife kitchen may even be better. The smaller versions marketed to American audiences generally have blades 7 to 8 inches long by a little more than 3 inches wide. They are made by every major knife manufacturer and are generally crafted from the same high-carbon stainless steel that the manufacturer uses for its other quality knives. The Dexter-Russell 8-inch cleaver is well crafted and easy to find in restaurant supply stores. Messermeister makes a nice midrange 8-inch cleaver for about $50. In any case, the thin blade is used just like a chef's knife. You can slice, dice, julienne, smash garlic, bone a chicken—whatever you need to do. The extra width of the blade is especially nice for scooping up piles of vegetables and transferring them to the pan.

If you are willing to be a little daring, a Chinese cleaver can do absolutely anything in the kitchen.

A Chinese cleaver is used a little differently than a chef's knife, but once you get used to the technique, you might want to consider a more traditional Chinese cleaver, called a *cai dou* by Chinese chefs and a *chukka bocho* by Japanese chefs. These are larger, have more rustic handles, and are almost always straight carbon steel rather than stainless. The very hard carbon steel can take an astonishingly sharp edge and hold it for a long time, but it does rust easily and discolors almost immediately in use.

Chinese cleavers are sometimes ranked by size from #1 to #4, with the #1 cleaver being the longest and widest. This numbering system doesn't include blade weight and thickness, so you have to look for clues. The thicker cleavers are called "choppers" and even "bone choppers" while the thinner ones are called "slicers" or "vegetable cleavers." That's what you're looking for. Your best bet is a slicer 8.5 to 9 inches by about 4.5 inches with a spine just a little thinner than a standard chef's knife. This is usually called a #3 slicer. There is some variability because most of the traditional Chinese cleavers are handmade. If you find a larger cleaver and like the way it feels, go for it. I find that the more delicate—if a chunk of steel this size can be called delicate—vegetable slicer is just about perfect for home use. Some chefs even prefer the smaller 7-inch by 3-inch slicer.

The more sophisticated and expensive Chinese cleavers are made in Japan, oddly enough. And just to make things complicated, the Japanese have their own numbering system. The equivalent to the standard #3 slicer in the Japanese system is a #6 cleaver. These chukka bocho range in price from $100 for a good-quality cleaver to more than $300, but even at the upper end of the price range there will be some variability in fit and finish. Whether you purchase a rough #3 slicer made in Hong Kong at an Asian market or buy a high-end chukka bocho from a specialty store, the focus will be on the performance of the knife rather than how it looks. Some Chinese cleavers are downright funky looking, so if you are very fussy about the looks of your knives, a traditional Chinese cleaver might not be for you. However, the Chinese have several thousand years of cooking experience on us and a high regard for knife skills. The weapon of choice for at least the last two thousand years has been the cleaver. That should tell you something.

A variant on the cleaver theme are Japanese vegetable knives. They are considerably narrower than Chinese cleavers, but the principle is the same: a thin-bladed, (usually) blunt-tipped knife designed for precision slicing. There are two basic styles, the nakiri and the usuba. Usuba means "thin knife" and nakiri works out to "knife for cutting edible leaves." Both knives are thin and both are used specifically for vegetables, so the terms are sometimes used interchangeably. In practice, however, they are differentiated by blade shape. The word "usuba" is used for the single-beveled restaurant-style version of this knife. An usuba generally has a higher level of fit and finish and greater heft. It has a thick spine just like the single-beveled yanagiba and deba.

The word "nakiri," on the other hand, usually connotes a more rustic double-beveled knife. It generally has a rounder front end, a much thinner spine, and is about half the weight of an usuba. It is a home cook's knife rather than a professional restaurant cook's knife. The nakiri is the only traditional Japanese blade with a *ryoba* (double-bevel) rather than a *kataba* (single-bevel) edge.

Both styles of knife are riding the wave of interest generated by the incredible sales of santokus in the United States. They aren't quite as prevalent as santokus, or even Chinese cleavers, but Messermeister, MAC, Kyocera, and Shun all have versions readily available with just a little searching.

SHEAR MADNESS: KITCHEN SHEARS

One more thing every knife block or drawer needs is a pair of heavy-duty kitchen shears. I'm not a big fan of the spring-loaded shears that look like tin snips. Those are usually marketed as poultry shears, but the regular scissors style works just fine for everything from cutting grapes from the stalk for school lunches to cutting the backbone out of a chicken. They even make short work of those miserable hard plastic clamshell packages that seem impervious to everything short of an industrial laser. A nifty trick is to use your shears as a pizza cutter, just like cutting construction paper for a fourth-grade class project. The sharp blades snip through the crust without squishing the toppings much better than wheel-on-a-stick pizza cutters. Look for shears that snap apart for easy cleaning.

POTTERY GONE WILD: CERAMICS

Ceramics are not technically a style of knife, I realize, but ceramic-bladed kitchen tools have made significant inroads in the market. Ceramic knives still haven't achieved their full potential, in my opinion. They are too light and too brittle for heavy use in the kitchen. Drop one on a hard kitchen floor and it is likely to shatter. Supporters say that they will keep their edge for an amazingly long time. That is true. Ceramic knives are very hard and the edge will not roll or wear. It will chip, however. More important, the factory edge isn't very sharp. It seems that the makers haven't quite figured out how to get the edge thin enough for maximum sharpness without crumbling. The ceramic knives I have sampled have all had disappointing edges right out of the box. That's usually fine. I'm used to factory edges not being as sharp as I would like. But with a ceramic blade you can't do anything about it. You cannot sharpen them yourself. They have to go back to the factory to be resharpened (to the same mediocre edge they came with). Avoid them. The technology isn't there yet.

On the other hand, ceramic blades are perfect for smaller

tools that don't rely on absolute sharpness, like peelers and mandoline slicers. In these applications, a ceramic blade is in its element. You rarely sharpen your mandoline or peeler blade anyway, and the blades are protected by plastic that only allows the food into a narrow slot, so ceramic's advantages outweigh its disadvantages. The ceramic blade will never rust and is much easier to clean than its steel counterpart. I have two ceramic Y peelers that are excellent, and now that I have a small paddle-shaped ceramic mandoline(ish) slicer, I'm ready to chuck my heavyweight mandoline. The mini-mandoline has notches at the far end that allow you to hook it directly over the top of a bowl and whittle a cucumber into perfect 2 mm rounds in a second or two. It's magic—and dishwasher safe.

3

A KNIFE FOR EVERY BUDGET

Good kitchen knives come in a variety of shapes and sizes. Luckily, they come at a variety of price ranges, too. The trick is finding the best knives for your budget. Let's look at several different scenarios. Remember, not all of the recommended knives will be available in all areas of the country. You may have to buy online.

THE INTERNET

If you have a local cutlery store, by all means patronize it if at all possible. Specialty stores offer a level of service, knowledge, and flexibility that you cannot find in any department store. Even high-end gourmet kitchenware stores receive their knife information mainly from manufacturers' representatives, so they may have a somewhat skewed view of what goes into making a great knife and what you should pay for it. A good specialty cutlery shop will usually be happy to special-order just about anything you can track down. They are probably as curious as you are about whatever nifty new knife you've read about. However, given the realities of shelf space, distribution, and profit margins, even the best cutlery store cannot get hold of every knife. That's where online shopping comes in.

Buying knives from online sources is a little problematic in that you cannot test-drive the knife to see how it feels in your hands. However, the better Internet knife stores have reasonable return policies, so as long as you don't do anything too drastic you can return a knife that isn't quite what you expected. You'll probably figure out whether or not a knife is for you within minutes of opening the box.

(Continued)

On the upside, the Internet is the great leveler, removing regional monopolies and price variations and opening up a vast array of great knives to those willing to poke around a little. You are no longer limited to what is available at the local strip mall. Besides, seeing the Brown Truck of Joy pull up outside is always a treat.

Here are some of my favorite sites:

Korin (www.korin.com)

Epicurean Edge (www.epicedge.com)

Korin and Epicurean Edge are two of the best knife stores on the Internet (or anywhere else). They both carry an exceptional range of high-quality knives. They might be a little pricier than some other stores, but the level of service, especially if you call or e-mail with questions, is worth it.

Other online knife and accessories stores worth seeking out:

Knife Outlet (www.knifeoutlet.com)

Knife Merchant (www.knifemerchant.com)

Japanese Chefs Knife (www.japanesechefsknife.com)

Broadway Panhandler (www.broadwaypanhandler.com)

Fantes Kitchen Wares (www.fantes.com)

Professional Cutlery Direct/Cooking Enthusiast (www.cutlery.com)

A. G. Russell Knives (www.agrussell.com)

Big Tray Restaurant Equipment (www.bigtray.com)

Chef Depot (www.chefdepot.com)

A Cook's Wares (www.cookswares.com)

The Japan Chef (www.thejapanchef.com)

There are many, many places to purchase knives on the Internet; I have only listed stores that I have direct experience with. I have purchased knives and equipment from each of these stores and would recommend them to friends.

For talk and information about kitchen knives, it is hard to beat the "In the Kitchen" section of Knife Forums (www.knifeforums.com) and "Fred's Cutlery Forum" at Foodie Forums (www.foodieforums.com). There are many knife discussion sites on the Internet, but these two are dedicated especially to kitchen knives. ▲

STARTER KITCHEN: FROM $25 TO $100

You might be equipping your first apartment kitchen and don't have a huge budget. Perhaps you need a good knife for your lake cabin or beach house and want something you won't feel bad about leaving behind at the end of the summer. Maybe you're sending your kid off to college with a minimal cooking kit in the hopes that he or she *might* actually eat something green every once in a while. Whatever the reason, if you need a good, inexpensive knife or two, you're in luck.

At about $25 at your local restaurant supply store, the Forschner/Victorinox 8-inch chef's knife (model 40520) is a bargain. The 10-inch version is just a couple of dollars more. Both are 2 inches at the heel, so be aware that they will not fit in all knife blocks. These are stamped knives, but Forschner, a division of Victorinox (the Swiss Army knife people), has come up with a chef's knife that largely circumvents the problems associated with stamped knives. The blade has some heft and reasonable rigidity. The Fibrox handle is comfortable and doesn't feel cheap and slippery like many of the similar-looking stamped knives you find in restaurant supply houses. Most important, though, the knife will take and hold a keen edge. Like many mass-produced knives, the Forschner chef's knives might need a quick swipe down a honing steel to remove any residual burr and line the edge up properly before use. The matching paring knife is about $5, so for approximately $30 you have a pair of knives that are as good as, if not better than, those found in most restaurant kitchens in America. Not bad for an afternoon's shopping.

If your budget allows for a little more flexibility and you are willing to buy a knife sight unseen, you are in for a real treat. Even at double the price of the Forschner, the Tojiro DP 210 mm gyuto is the bargain of the century. The 240 mm (9.5-inch) version is about $10 more. The Tojiro DP has a thin inner core of extremely hard stain-resistant steel jacketed

The Forschner/Victorinox chef's knife is an excellent starter knife.

by a layer of softer stainless on the outside. The hard inner core gives you a very sharp, long-lasting edge. However, very hard steel can be brittle. The softer outer jacket provides some toughness in case the knife gets dropped or banged around. It also makes sharpening easier because you are only dealing with a thin strip of hard steel at the edge. The Tojiro DP line is rarely seen in U.S. stores, even specialty cutlery shops, but has developed a rabid following via Internet sales as one of the best entry-level high-performance knives around. The quality of the handle fit can be a little variable, and the handles themselves are blocky, but the performance of these knives is outstanding, especially for the price. Togiharu knives, sold through Korin (see Resources), includes a line priced comparably to the Tojiro DP but with better construction and higher quality steel.

Paring knives can be surprisingly expensive. Prices upwards of $50 are not unusual for a 3.5-inch parer, but there are very few quality paring knives in the no-man's land between the $5 plastic-handled knives and the $50-and-up range. There are a couple of strategies for procuring a small knife for an equally small outlay. You could simply purchase a cheap paring knife or two at the local restaurant supply store or kitchenware outlet and consider them disposable items. These knives usually have molded plastic handles, sometimes in bright colors, and are sufficient to get you through a week at the beach but don't hold up well with long-term use.

In the middle range, however, there are three true standouts, and for about $30 you can bring home a paring knife that will last for the rest of your cooking life. In this price range, the MAC 3.25-inch paring knife (PKF-30), part of MAC's Professional series, demonstrates why working chefs (who have to buy their own knives) like MAC knives. It is a solid workhorse paring knife with good ergonomics, great steel, and a long-lasting, aggressive edge. Again, MAC knives are hard to find in retail stores, but a little surfing will hook you up in short order. If you have a gourmet shop or cutlery store nearby, take a close look at Wüsthof-Trident's *Le Cordon Bleu* line of knives. Designed in conjunction with the famed cooking school, these knives have a collar-style bolster that doesn't go all the way down the heel, making them much easier to sharpen and maintain. The paring knife in this series is a steal. In the same vein, Messermeister's Meridian Elité series features a half bolster for lighter weight and easier sharpening. The 3.5-inch paring knife is a couple of dollars more than the Cordon Bleu from Wüsthof, but is more sturdily constructed. The Meridian Elité series knives come with a particularly refined edge that far surpasses those on the better-known German brands.

There you have it: even with limited funds you can own a decent chef's knife that will get you cooking in style. Match that to one of the suggested paring knives and add a $15 bread knife from the local restaurant supply store and you've got the Big Three covered quite nicely. Stretch just a little bit for a better chef's knife and you have an unbeatable starter set that will last as long as you need it to—or until you are ready to make a larger investment in your knives—and we're still under $100.

BUDGET GOURMET: FROM $100 TO $200

If you can extend your budget just a little farther you can outfit your kitchen with souped-up versions of the Big Three and have a set of knives that would do any chef proud. The Tojiro and Togiharu gyuto/chef's knives mentioned above hold their own in this price range, but the field has expanded dramatically. There is a wide array of 8-inch chef's knives available for $80 to $100, including many of the better-known brands found in every kitchenware store. Those are indeed fine choices, but if you are interested in the best performance at the best price, three knives truly stand out, two from the now-familiar MAC and Messermeister lines and one from the Japanese company that started the revolution toward thinner, lighter knives, Global. All three are on the budget end of our price scale and on the extreme upper end of the performance scale. They are the Global G2 8-inch cook's knife, the MAC 8-inch dimpled chef's knife (MTH-80), and the Messermeister Meridian Elité chef's knife. These three knives effectively redefine the classic 8-inch chef's knife.

The chef's knife redefined: Messermeister Meridian Elité, Global G2, and MAC MTH-80.

Like the PKF-30 paring knife above, the MAC MTH-80 is from the Professional series and is a treat to use. The Professional series knives have graceful lines and feature welded-on bolsters to add a little heft to the knife. The MTH-80 has a Granton-like edge with oval kullens hollowed into the blade. This theoretically keeps food from sticking, but the effect is limited at best. That doesn't change the fact that this knife is a cutting machine. Both it and the Global feel light and nimble in the hands. MAC has built its reputation in professional kitchens rather than kitchenware stores. They are extremely popular among chefs and line cooks because they are comfortable, reasonably priced, high-quality knives that come with an aggressive edge and hold it for a very long time.

Global is credited for revolutionizing the kitchen knife market in the mid-1980s, introducing American cooks to thin, lightweight, razor-sharp Japanese-made knives for the first time and challenging the "full forged with a bolster" mantra that salespeople repeat zombielike in gourmet shops across the country. The stippled stainless-steel handles are a love 'em or hate 'em affair. There is little middle ground. The knife itself is light, lively, and fun to use. Unlike many Japanese-made knives, which tend to be a little blade heavy, the Global G2 is neutrally balanced at the transition between the blade and the handle.

Messermeister has two premier lines, Meridian Elité and San Moritz Elité. The difference is the handle. The Meridian Elité knives have a standard three-rivet handle; the San Moritz knives have a molded handle. What distinguishes these knives from most other German knives is their partial bolsters and the polished edges. Because the bolster does not go all the way to the edge on the Elité knives, they are considerably easier to sharpen. Knives with full bolsters can develop a half moon–shaped notch just forward of the heel because the thick bolster changes the angle of the edge during sharpening. This happens over time but is especially problematic when electric sharpeners are used too often or too aggressively. This swale (as the notch is sometimes called) prevents the heel of the knife from fully connecting with the cutting board, making the back portion of the knife virtually useless unless it is ground out. The Elité knives also come with an acute, highly polished edge, making them extremely potent cutters. Having spent a long afternoon peering at knife edges under a high-powered microscope I can say that Messermeister's Elité knives come with the best factory edge of any of the big-name knife brands.

The MAC and Global knives are lightweight and nimble in the hands. The Messermeister, like most Western knives, is weightier and more deliberate. For traditionalists, the

Messermeister is hard to beat. For the slightly more fashionable, the Global chef's knife makes a bold statement. The MAC will outcut just about any knife out there. Remember, these are the 8-inch chef's knives. The 9-inch, 240 mm (approximately 9.5 inches), and 10-inch versions will be slightly more expensive but well worth the investment.

At this price point many manufacturers offer a discounted starter set consisting of a chef's knife and paring knife. These are often very good deals and are especially nice if you don't like the look of mismatched knives. As an example, Shun knives, with their beautiful swirled faux-Damascus steel blades, are usually a little pricey for this budget level. However, their two-piece starter set—consisting of an 8-inch chef's knife and 3.5-inch paring knife in a bamboo box—is frequently discounted to about $150. That paring knife (the Shun DM0700), by the way, is everything a paring knife should be. It is just under $50 at most kitchenware stores. Add that to the Messermeister, Wüsthof Cordon Bleu, and MAC parers and we have a small knife to fit every hand. One thing to note: the Shun knives have oval handles with a ridge running down the right side. The blade is also slightly off center to the left. Both of these features are designed to accommodate a right hand. If you are a lefty you may have to special order.

With this budget you can now afford a really good bread knife. There are two in particular, the 10-inch Wüsthof Super Slicer and the MAC 10.5-inch SB-105 bread/roast slicer. Both have "reverse" scalloped edges, which means that, unlike serrated knives, they can double as meat slicers. Wüsthof makes a Super Slicer in each of its product lines, but the best value is the Wüsthof Gourmet version. This, like the MAC, is a stamped blade with no bolster, but both are attractive enough to reside happily alongside snootier knives. Each is about $50, so even with the most expensive chef's knife and paring knife in this price range, we are still under $200 total.

Mix and match any of these choices to make up your Big Three triumvirate.

THE BIG UPGRADE

If you have outgrown the knives you purchased when you got your first apartment or the set you received as a wedding gift and are looking to move up in the world, get out the checkbook. There is an amazing array of high-quality kitchen knives available, but once you get past the Big Three things can get expensive, especially if you go nuts and buy a twenty-two-piece set of knives in a gigantic block. All those pretty matching handles may look great next to the new hot-rod gas range and flashy sauté pans, but you will never use the majority of the knives. Given that some of these sets can run upwards of $1,500, that's a lot of wasted money and wasted counter space.

However, there is a certain appeal to a owning a matching set of knives. You already know how to mix and match within a set to get exactly what you want and need (see page 14). As a reminder, when buying knives in a set there are a couple of things to look out for. The shears that come with many sets are not the manufacturer's best. Trade out a redundant knife or just pay the difference to get the higher-grade shears. Messermeister's take-apart shears are truly excellent and should be the standard by which others are judged. Also remember to swap out the coarse- or medium-grooved steel that comes with many sets for a fine steel at the very least. A ceramic honing rod would be even better.

At the $250-and-up price point, there is some good news and some bad news. The very good news is that you can expand beyond—even far beyond—the Big Three. The sky is the limit. And if you really, really want your knives to match, you can do that, too. Have fun. And despite what I said earlier, if you have the budget and the desire for the multithousand-dollar enormo-block with more pieces than the London

Philharmonic (with mango slicer!), go for it. No one gets hurt.

The bad news is that it is still very easy to spend a lot of money on mediocre knives. Even if you have money to burn, there is no reason to burn it on poor performers.

The justly famous Wüsthof-Trident knives and the Messermeister Meridian/San Moritz Elité brands represent the best of the German knife camps. The Wüsthof Classic line has dominated the cutlery industry for years but the Cordon Bleu line is a lighter-weight alternative with partial bolsters and more polished edges. The eight-piece Cordon Bleu set comes with an 8-inch offset deli knife in place of the less useful 8-inch straight bread knife. We've already discussed the features and benefits of the Messermeister knives. They are as good in bulk as they are individually. Both manufacturers offer an assortment of prepackaged knife sets or mix-and-match open stock. If you like German knives, either choice is fine. The Wüsthofs have more snob appeal. The Messermeisters have better edges and more comfortable handles.

On the American side of the Atlantic, Chef's Choice, better known for its electric sharpeners, makes a great line of cutlery. The Chef's Choice Trizor 10X knives have a much higher carbon content than comparable knives and are hardened to about 60 on the Rockwell C scale. Most commercially available knives are hardened to 52 to 56 Rockwell. The Chef's Choice knives will stay sharp significantly longer in use. They come with an edge that is fatter than I'd like, but it is no worse than most. Because the steel is so hard, the edge can be sharpened to a much more acute angle with little or no fear of damage, if you are so inclined. They also have a sharply tapered bolster that flattens to next to nothing at the heel, which allows you to sharpen the full length of the edge. The Chef's Choice knives are designed along German lines with a pronounced belly on the chef's knives. These knives are hefty and substantial and come with equally hefty price tags. A five-piece set (counting a knife block) is just under $450. If you like Western styling but want better steel and more comfortable handles, the Chef's Choice knives certainly justify the price.

Straddling the line between European and Japanese design is the Shun brand from Kai/Kershaw. The chef's knives have a belly sweep like German knives, but the blades are thin, lightweight, and hard like Japanese knives. Shun knives are made in Seki City, one of Japan's traditional knife-making centers. The Shun Classic line of knives has an inner core of VG10 steel covered with an outer jacket of softer steel made up of sixteen layers that have been folded and welded into a lovely pattern of swirls and waves called *suminigashi* or "ink pattern" because it resembles an ancient Japanese paper-decorating technique of the same name where drops of ink were carefully dripped into still water and blown into swirls.

Shun knives blend Western and Japanese qualities.

Shun knives have an oval handle with a ridge running down the right side. The blades are also slightly offset to the left—if you look down at one from the top, the blade does not come out of the center of the handle but a little to the left of center to accommodate your right forefinger in a Pinch grip. Which is fine if you are right handed. Many lefties never even notice the difference. For those who do, Shun knives are available in left-handed versions that may involve special ordering. The shape of the handle is similar to traditional Japanese knives. The ridge theoretically keeps the knife from twisting in your hand, but I have not noticed that it has any significant effect in use. If your knife is rotating in your hand, you are gripping it incorrectly. Shun knives are expensive, even for this budget range. Just remember that you don't need every knife that a manufacturer produces. Start with the basics and work your way up as needed.

If Shun mixes European and Japanese elements, MAC and Global knives are firmly on the Japanese side though they are still recognizably designed for Western cooks. The MAC Professional and Global knives we were discussing earlier easily hold their own here in the upper ranges of the price stratosphere. You can just buy more of them for the same money.

Globals and Shuns are easy to find. They are often sold at the same stores that carry Wüsthofs, Henckels, and other well-known brands. This gives you a chance to test-drive them, even if it is in a limited fashion. Better stores will have a cutting board on hand and allow you to at least simulate cutting something up. Chef's Choice, MAC, and Messermeister don't have the advertising budgets or shelf space of the others so they can be a little harder to track down in retail stores. Their performance advantages make it well worth it to seek them out, though, either at a specialty cutlery shop or online. All of the brands mentioned are readily available with a little effort on your part. Kitchenware stores, specialty cutlery retailers, and Internet knife stores will happily sell you a matched set in a convenient knife block or allow you to mix and match open stock to suit your needs. That's what this price point is all about.

If having matching handles is not that important, you could also . . .

GET FUNKY

This section is not so much a price point or budget level as it is a lifestyle. If you tend to be a little unconventional or if you even *think* that you might be a kitchen knife enthusiast, reconcile yourself to the idea that you'll be amassing a small collection of high-performance knives, no two alike and each one purchased for a specific reason or to fulfill a particular desire. If you really like kitchen knives, you are going to end up at this point anyway. You might as well save some money and anguish along the way. For some people knives are like pots and pans. They are tools, and it is nice to have good ones. For others, me included, great kitchen knives are an end unto themselves. We will search out recipes involving a lot of knife work just to have an excuse to use our knives. Mismatched handles are a badge of honor. Steel composition is debated as wine lovers argue about grape varieties or the rainfall in Bordeaux. If you don't have a tight budget, are bored by the Big Three, or don't mind piecemealing your knife collection (which is what it will become over time), go ahead and start wading into the deep end of the pool. The water is fine.

> **Cooks, at least serious cooks, can be roughly divided into two major groups: pot cooks and knife cooks. Of course, each sort uses both implements; it is a matter of which serves as the lodestone of their kitchen—the piece of cookware that, in case of a fire, they would run to rescue first. There is no doubt that I am a knife cook. While I may have always yearned for the right pot, I actually needed the right knife to find myself as a cook. Even today, if I reached under the counter and found my favorite pot missing, I would groan, yes, but I would have no trouble using another one. Take away my knife, however, and all my kitchen skills would go flitting out the window.**
>
> —JOHN THORNE, *Pot on the Fire: Further Exploits of a Renegade Cook*

You could start by simply mixing and matching among the knives already mentioned in the previous categories. It would be very hard to go wrong with any of them. You can put together a spectacular set of knives, one or two at a time, secure in the knowledge that you are indeed purchasing the best knives for your hands, your cooking style, and your budget.

On the other hand, if you are the exploratory type, there is a wide, wide world of high-performance kitchen knives out there, though few of them are available through regular gourmet or kitchen stores. The Internet is your friend. Sometimes that means wading through clunky online ordering systems or deciphering poorly translated product descriptions. That's part of the fun. Even more fun is when the package arrives. It is like sending presents to yourself. And if a new purchase doesn't turn out to be the gem you'd hoped for, there are other enthusiasts who will happily take it off your hands. You just have to keep in mind that some of the best-performing knives on the planet can be, well, rustic, to say the least. Others are as lovely and polished as a vintage Bentley (and nearly as expensive). These knives can be exotic, but are still "off the rack." Custom-made knives are another matter entirely. Many of the knives you will encounter if you choose to go the eclectic enthusiast route are produced by small Japanese companies. Good brands to look out for include Hattori, Misono, Masamoto, Glestain, Ryusen, Suisin, Mizuno Tanrenjyo, Shigefusa, Kikuichi, Artisan, and Nenox. If you were intrigued by the discussion of gyutos earlier, these are the folks who can hook you up.

Bread-loving knife fans get all misty-eyed over the hand-made bread knives of Franz Güde and the Grandmoulin bread knife from German manufacturer Herder, both in the knife-making center of Solingen. Vintage carbon-steel Sabatier and Nogent knives from France are also popular among knife cognoscenti. The obsession is not exactly like collecting obscure British sports cars or rare tulip bulbs, but it is not as different as you might think, either.

CUSTOM-MADE KITCHEN KNIVES

If you long for knives that are truly yours and yours alone, you'll want to look into custom-made kitchen knives. This is not as outlandish as it sounds. While there are certainly some expensive options out there, great custom knives can be had for about the same price as you'd pay for the more pedestrian stuff at the local kitchen store. There are literally thousands of knife makers out there but relatively few of them specialize in kitchen knives.

The American Bladesmith Society (ABS) is an organization dedicated to preserving and promoting the art and science of forging knives in the traditional manner. There are fewer than 100 knife makers who have passed its rigorous Master's test. Two of them make kitchen knives. ABS Master Bladesmiths Murray Carter and Bob Kramer are some of the most in-demand makers of fine kitchen cutlery around.

Murray Carter is a Canadian who learned traditional knife making in Japan, becoming the first non-Japanese ever to be invited to join one of the ancient bladesmithing families. After fifteen years in Japan, he relocated to the United States. His knives are firmly in the Japanese tradition and come with some of the sharpest edges any cook has ever seen. Write or e-mail for a catalog.

Murray Carter

Carter Cutlery

P.O. Box 307

Vernonia, OR 97064

503-429-0447

carter.cutlery@verizon.net

www.cartercutlery.com

Bob Kramer spent ten years in professional kitchens before changing careers and becoming a knife maker, earning his ABS Master rating in 1997. His experience shows in the agile handling and keen edges of his chef's knives.

(Continued)

Kramer Knives
6245A Rich Road SE
Olympia, WA 98501
360-455-4357
jambwa@earthlink.net
www.kramerknives.com

Thomas Haslinger is another former chef turned knife maker. His knives are ground from high-tech steel rather than forged. He has an extremely innovative design for chef's knives.

Thomas Haslinger
164 Fairview Drive SE
Calgary, Alberta
Canada T2H 1B3
403-253-9628
thomas@haslinger-knives.com
www.haslinger-knives.com

George Tichbourne is not a chef but he did design his line of kitchen knives in conjunction with some of Canada's top chefs.

George Tichbourne
7035 Maxwell Road, #5
Mississauga, Ontario
Canada L5S 1R5
905-670-0200
sales@tichbourneknives.com
www.tichbourneknives.com

Phil Wilson is renowned for his fillet knives, but he also makes top-notch chef's knives.

Seamount Knifeworks
info@seamountknifeworks.com
www.seamountknifeworks.com

An up-and-coming maker of chef's and kitchen knives, Lloyd "Butch" Harner has some interesting designs.

butch@harnerknives.com
www.harnerknives.com

Ray Rogers also makes some innovative fillet and chef's knives.

Ray Rogers
P.O. Box 126
Wauconda, WA 98859
knives@rayrogers.com
www.rayrogers.com

When contacting a custom knife maker you may have to deal with clunky Web sites and irregular schedules. Do not let that deter you. Each of these makers will be happy to discuss the knives they have in stock that might fit your needs or crafting a knife to your wants and needs. It's generally better to peruse their Web sites and e-mail first before making a phone call. They are generally one-man operations and every minute they spend on the phone is another minute away from the forge or grinder. ▲

4

THE OTHER HALF OF THE EQUATION: CUTTING BOARDS AND STORAGE

Now that you have a knife or two (or ten), you still are only halfway there. You need a cutting board. Actually, you need at least two cutting boards, but we'll get to that in a minute. Let's start with what *not* to cut on. Glass, ceramic, granite, and stainless steel are all no-no's. They will damage your edges. There is a special place in hell for people who abuse their knives this way. Countertops are also a bad idea. If your countertop surface is harder than your knife—granite, for example—you will damage the knife. If the countertop material is softer, you'll leave cuts in the countertop. Neither will win you any points with your spouse or the Kitchen Gods (who are *always* watching).

CUTTING BOARD BASICS

You need at least two, one for fruits, vegetables, bread, and anything that is safe to be eaten raw. Let's call this one your ready-to-eat board. Even though the items you cut on it

THE FBI (FOODBORNE ILLNESSES)

Background

There are thousands of viruses and pathogens and millions of bacteria swarming in, on, and around us at all times. *E. coli*, as a matter of fact, is a natural and necessary inhabitant of the intestines of nearly all animals, including people. Don't want to deal with it? Get yourself a big plastic bubble and a sleeping bag. Otherwise, just accept the fact that we're surrounded by bacteria, most of which we will never need to worry about, and get on with your life.

The Bad News

The bad bugs *are* out there. You've probably already run into them. There's no such thing as a "24-hour stomach flu," so that long night you spent endlessly counting your bathroom floor tiles was probably food poisoning of one sort or another. The Centers for Disease Control estimate that there are between 76 and 81 million cases of food poisoning each year, the vast majority of which go unreported because they didn't require a trip to the hospital or doctor's office.

Foodborne illnesses kill between 5,000 and 9,000 people each year, mostly the very young, the very old, and those with compromised immune systems. If you are cooking for someone who falls into this category, you need to take extra precautions to prevent cross-contamination in your kitchen. Most people suffer mild to severe diarrhea, fever, nausea, vomiting, and abdominal pain, and get well on their own in about a week. About 325,000 cases are serious enough to require hospitalization.

And the Really Bad News . . .

Somewhere between 80 and 90 percent of food poisoning incidents can be traced to food prepared and eaten at home.

Wash Your Hands

Common kitchen pathogens include *Salmonella*, *Campylobacter jejuni*, and the ever popular *E. coli*, along with a whole host of other bacteria, viruses, molds, fungi, and parasites.

(Continued)

While *E. coli* 0157:H7 gets a lot of press, *Campylobacter* is by far the most common source of food poisoning.

Hand washing is the best preventive. Eighty percent of all pathogens are spread through hand contact. Every 60 seconds a working adult touches as many as thirty objects. The number of people who *say* they don't wash their hands or cutting boards after cutting raw meat or chicken has dropped to 15 percent in recent years. Those are the mouth-breathers who admit it. Videotaped studies of kitchen habits show that the real number is about 30 percent. That is just scary. Knowing how to minimize cross-contamination is vital. Hands, sinks, sponges, and cutting boards are prime bacteria delivery systems. Sinks and sponges are the worst offenders. Cutting boards, because they come in contact with a variety of foods during a single meal preparation, have got to be kept clean to avoid transferring pathogens from one food item to the next. That's why you need one board that is just for meats, fish, and poultry. A recent report found that 80 percent of all grocery-store chickens in the United States are contaminated with *Salmonella, Campylobacter,* or both. You don't want that in your salad or on your strawberry shortcake.

"But," you say, "my grandmother/mother/aunt used the same cutting board forever and never gave it anything more than a quick wipe down. We never got sick." Maybe. Times are different now. Your grandmother's fish and chicken came from a neighbor or the next county over. Even grocery stores were stocked with relatively local ingredients farmed on a moderate scale. Today's factory-farmed chickens, tasty as they might be, are inbred mutants with more recessive genes than the royal family. Your leafy greens were picked under conditions that in no way resemble those in your grandmother's garden. Wash your hands. And your cutting board.*

*See "Cutting Board Sanitation" (page 91) to find out how to do it properly. ▲

might be ingredients in another dish and might even end up cooked, they can all safely be eaten as is without cooking. The other board is specifically (and solely) for raw meats, poultry, and fish. This is absolutely critical. There are some strategies for using just one cutting board in a home kitchen, but they are compromises at best. You need two cutting boards. End of story.

You have a bit of leeway with your ready-to-eat board—it can be as large as you like—but for your meat/poultry board, get the largest cutting board you can stand upright in your sink. Being able to rinse the board with flowing water is extremely important. A cutting board 15 inches by 20 inches is about the functional limit for most household sinks, and that's pushing it. However, you need as much size as you can get to prevent stuff running off onto your countertops.

I have one board that is dedicated to poultry alone. As much as I like chicken, there are enough risks associated with handling it raw that it gets isolated like Hannibal Lecter.

Cutting boards come in three major categories: wood (including bamboo and wood fiber composites), plastic (polypropylene and high-density polyethylene), and hard rubber. Wood and hard rubber boards have better tactile feedback. They feel better to cut on and, in a busy kitchen, are faster than plastic. On the downside, rubber boards can be grabby, causing your knife edge to catch a little on the way through your lovely red pepper julienne.

THE ONE-BOARD COMPROMISE

Let me repeat, you really should use two cutting boards. If, however, you are in a situation where that is impractical, there is a technique for using one cutting board reasonably safely. Think through everything you will be making and prep the items in order of contamination risk and cooking temperature: fruits and vegetables first, fish and low-temperature meats (medium-rare steaks, for example) second, and poultry last. Cutting a head of lettuce after butterflying a couple of chicken breasts is just playing Russian Roulette with your gastrointestinal tract. You might as well lick the raw chicken. It *will* catch up to you sooner or later.

When you are done, be sure to clean your cutting board thoroughly before putting anything else on it. Cooked food should never be put back onto a board that has held raw food unless the board has been properly scrubbed in hot soapy water. ▲

Plastic or poly boards can be hard on knife edges. They feel "crunchy" when you try to cut quickly on them. On the other hand, poly boards are inexpensive and dishwasher safe, and come in colors. Professional kitchens use color-coded boards to prevent cross-contamination: white for dairy products, green for vegetables, blue for seafood, yellow for raw poultry, and red for raw meat. This is a great way to avoid cross-contamination of foods and is a major plus for the plastic boards.

Wood and hard rubber boards (Sani-Tuff brand boards specifically) can be resurfaced by sanding. Plastic/poly boards cannot. Hand-sanding a plastic cutting board leaves a surface that is more scratched and scarred than when you started. And if you try to use a powered sander, the plastic melts and shreds. Not fun.

With wood cutting boards you have two basic choices, end grain or edge grain. End-grain boards look like checkerboards. They are made by jointing and gluing many small blocks of wood together with the cut ends facing upwards. They are sometimes called butcher blocks. The vertical grain makes for a surface that is extremely durable and is easier on your knives than edge-grain or plastic boards. End-grain boards are more expensive than other types of cutting boards. They are usually much thicker, too. This can be a blessing or a curse depending on how tall you are. Standard kitchen countertops are 36 inches high. A really thick cutting board or one with feet on the bottom can make it feel like your elbows are up around your ears when you try to cut something. I have a 3.5-inch-thick butcher block board, which puts the cutting surface just under 40 inches from the ground. That is about the limit of comfort for anyone under 6 feet tall.

Big, butcher block–style cutting boards are wonderful but are so large that they cannot be cleaned as effectively as smaller boards. If you have one, it should be your ready-to-eat board. Fruits, veggies, cheese, bread, and such. No meat. No fish. Definitely no poultry.

Edge-grain boards are made by placing planks of wood on edge (taller than they are wide) and gluing them together under pressure. You can tell an edge grain board by the stripes. Edge-grain boards are not as strong as end-grain boards but they cost significantly less. They are also a lot easier to store and move around the kitchen. Neither type of wood board should ever go through the dishwasher.

Wood cutting boards should be made from hard, tightly grained woods like hard rock maple, walnut, cherry, teak, bamboo, ash, or birch.

There are two specialty cutting board materials that also deserve some recognition: composite fiber and hard rubber. Cutting boards sold under the Epicurean brand are made from a wood-and-paper-fiber composite called Richlite. Other cutting board manufacturers have started making composite cutting boards from Richlite as well. These cutting boards are durable, dishwasher safe, relatively heatproof (you can use them as trivets), and nonporous. They are also very lightweight. I use one as my travel board. I take it (along with a couple of knives) whenever I cook somewhere other than my own kitchen. There are only two downsides that I have found. The composite fiber material is harder than nonlaminated wood, so they roll the edges of your knives more easily than a standard wood board, and they are so lightweight and smooth that they tend to slide around on the countertop. A damp towel underneath will fix that. It is always a good idea to stabilize your cutting board anyway. As for your edges, if you use a composite fiber cutting board you may have to steel your knives more often. But you are already doing that, right? Right?

Hard rubber cutting boards are also something of a specialty item. Like plastic boards, they can be run through the dishwasher, though they should be removed before the drying cycle to prevent warping. Unlike plastic boards, rubber boards do not fracture or create fissures when cut. These cutting boards, sold through restaurant supply stores under the Sani-Tuff brand, are very heavy duty. The don't slide around at all on the countertop. On the other hand, they are a bear to haul around the kitchen. They combine many of the positive attributes of wood boards with many of the positive attributes of plastic boards. The downsides are the weight, the color (a sickly industrial beige), and the price. They are more expensive than edge-grain wood boards but less expensive than end-grain boards.

WOOD VERSUS PLASTIC

If you do any reading about cutting boards, you'll run across the wood versus plastic debate almost immediately. Faulty interpretation of some scientific research led to a widespread belief that wood has natural antibacterial properties. It doesn't. Despite a lot of hype and misguided news reports, wood does not have any magical germ-killing abilities—unless you find capillary action magical. It *is* pretty cool.

Wood does not kill off bacteria and/or pathogens. It absorbs them. The bugs, bacteria, and nasties are sucked into the first millimeter or so of the wood and are trapped there. They generally live a couple of hours. How you feel about this is up to you. Technically, these bacteria *are* recoverable through destructive testing or aggressive laboratory sampling. That means that they are still a threat—in theory—to any foods placed on the cutting board. In practice, they do not transfer to knife edges or cross-contaminate other foods because the board will not let go of them. They stay trapped in the wood and die as the board dries.

Dry wood boards absorb pathogens. Wet wood boards do not; they act just like wet plastic boards. Bacteria and other bugs are readily recoverable from both wood and plastic when wet. Treating the wood board with mineral oil or wax may make it more impermeable, reducing the absorption effect. The evidence is mixed.

WOOD VS. PLASTIC: GEEKSPEAK

One of the very few case-controlled studies of sporadic salmonellosis included cutting boards among the many risk factors assessed. Although the effects were less significant than other risk factors, the study revealed that those using wooden cutting boards in their home kitchens were less than half as likely on average to contract salmonellosis; those using synthetic (plastic or glass) cutting boards were about twice as likely on average to contract salmonellosis. ▲

So what about plastic and poly cutting boards? New plastic boards are easy to clean and sanitize. Bacteria don't penetrate the surface and can be washed away easily. The problem comes when the cutting board becomes scarred (which happens much more readily than with wood boards). Knife scars on plastic boards are not clean incisions. The cuts fracture, creating a microscopic web of fissures below the surface. These fissures create a safe harbor for bacteria. It becomes more and more difficult to remove the pathogens through hand washing. These fissures also can hold on to moisture, creating a friendly environment for bacteria. While scarred plastic boards become harder and harder to sanitize, knife-scarred wood boards act just like new wood boards. There is little or no difference in their ability to absorb and trap pathogens. In either wood or plastic boards, bacteria and pathogens are tenacious and create an anchor film that resists anything less than vigorous scrubbing. That's why it is so important to clean them properly. With a plastic or poly board, that may be as simple as putting it in the dishwasher, which is verboten for wood cutting boards.

CUTTING BOARD SANITATION

The type of cutting board you use is significantly less important than knowing how to clean it.

If you are washing by hand (as you should be with wood cutting boards), wash your cutting board before any other dishes or after washing everything else. An initial scrub and rinse prior to washing makes more difference in pathogen reduction than any other step you take. You want to rinse the board before putting anything else in the sink, or after everything else is done so you don't contaminate your wash water or other dishes. Putting your contaminated cutting board into a sink full of warm, soapy water just gets you a sink full of warm, soapy, contaminated water that may then contaminate everything else you wash.

Hard-flowing water is critical. Give your cutting board a good rinse and rubdown with a dishcloth or scrub brush. Either is fine. Dishcloths are rough enough to scrub your cutting board well. Unlike sponges, they also tend to dry out before growing high numbers of bacteria. That's part of the reason sponges have been banished from my house; they are like little germ spas. Scrub brushes are easy to clean and don't retain microorganisms after rinsing. Whichever method you use, a good rinse and scrub will eliminate most of the bacteria and pathogens that might be contaminating your cutting board.

After the initial plain water scrub, wash your cutting board in hot soapy water. Be aware that the heat of the water does not kill germs. Water hot enough to kill germs will send you to the emergency room. However, fats and oils can provide a protective coating for bacteria, a way for them to survive even moderate scrubbing. Hot water aids the cleaning effect of dish soaps in removing grease and fats that can safeguard bacteria under them. When you are done, rinse the cutting board thoroughly and let it air-dry. That's it. No magic formulas or harsh chemicals.

If you are the belt and suspenders type (I am), or if you are cooking for a small child, an elderly person, or anyone with a weakened immune system, you might want to take an additional precautionary step. To kill the last of the bad bugs, keep a 25 percent solution of vinegar in a spray bottle—¼ cup of vinegar to ¾ cup of water or thereabouts. Spray down your cutting boards and stand them upright in the dish drainer to air-dry. I use vinegar because I have cutting boards in a variety of materials. The commonly recommended dilute bleach solutions are not as effective on wood cutting boards. Wood boards neutralize the free oxygen in bleach, negating its germ-fighting abilities. Vinegar works on every type of board. Vinegar does work a little more slowly than bleach, but is just as effective, especially since the acetic acid in vinegar concentrates as it dries, making it an even more potent germ fighter.

Neither vinegar nor bleach will do you a bit of good on a grubby cutting board. The vast majority of the debugging occurs during cleaning. Trying to sanitize a dirty board is futile, as is simply wiping down your cutting board with a bleach-soaked rag. Scrubbing is the key. The sanitizing step is just added insurance. Either way, flood the board thoroughly and allow it to air-dry upright.

Plastic, hard rubber, and composite wood (Richlite) cutting boards can be washed in the dishwasher, which is fairly effective for cleaning and sanitizing (not sterilizing) them. However, the dishwasher is even more effective if it has a sanitize cycle and you have adjusted your water heater to accommodate it. Your dishwasher needs to hit at least 140 degrees Fahrenheit. You can help the process along by running the hot water in your kitchen sink until it hits its peak temperature prior to starting the washer. Even if you are using the dishwasher, you still need to give the board a good scrub and rinse first. There's nothing like real physical friction to get rid of the goo.

If you do use the dishwasher, pull your cutting boards out before the drying cycle, which can warp them. Whether you use the dishwasher or hand wash, stand the board on end and let it dry. Air flow is important. Let your cutting boards dry completely before stacking or putting them away in cabinets or you'll just trap moisture and bacteria. Drying alone is effective at reducing bacteria and pathogens.

When plastic boards become scarred enough to snag your dishcloth when washing, throw them away. You cannot sand them down. They just melt. When wood boards reach the same stage (snagging the cloth), sand them down or see if your local cabinet shop will run them through their thickness planer for you. Sanding out the knife scars doesn't make the cutting board any more antipathogenic. Even a smooth wood surface looks like the canals of Mars to bacteria. It does, however, make the cutting board easier to clean and less likely to harbor big bits of nastiness that are hard to dislodge. A smoother surface is also safer to cut on.

In addition to rigid cutting boards, there are numerous flexible cutting boards out there too. There are two types, neither ideal. The one-use disposable paper cutting mats sold in grocery stores aren't quite heavy duty enough in my opin-

---

CLEANING YOUR BUTCHER BLOCK

If you are fortunate enough to have a large butcher block or even a heavy butcher block–style cutting board, it is probably too big to fit in your sink. That's why it should be your ready-to-eat board. Cleaning can be as simple as scraping it down with a bench scraper or wiping it down with a clean, damp dishcloth. However, if you cut a lot of onions and garlic, your butcher block will trap their odors. Or if you do need to cut meat or poultry on your butcher block, you need a way to clean and sanitize it. There is an old butcher's trick that works for both situations. Make a thick paste of salt (I use kosher because the larger crystals are easier to work with) and a little water. After wiping the surface as best you can, rub the paste on your butcher block, scrubbing it in thoroughly with your hands. Let the salt paste dry overnight. It will absorb the smell of the garlic and onions. It will also kill off any pathogens. They are not salt tolerant. Scrape the dried salt off in the morning with a bench scraper. (A bench scraper is a handy tool to have around. Sometimes called a dough scraper or dough knife, the wide, square blade is ideal for scooping stuff off your board or scraping off stuck bits of food.) If you want to be doubly sure about your butcher block's sanitation, give it a spritz from your diluted vinegar solution. ▲

---

ion. Some have fold-up edges to keep juices and chicken goo from running off. That's all well and good, except that is very easy to cut through them, leaving juices and goo (and knife scars) on the countertops. Not good. I could see using these for picnics or in an RV or camper where washing up is more problematic. Otherwise, avoid them.

Flexible plastic cutting mats are big items in housewares stores. Some even come in color-coded packs. These are sturdier than the disposable paper cutting mats, but are still prone to scarring. On the upside, they are easy to clean in the dishwasher, convenient for moving foods from the counter to a pot on the stove, and make switching mats for different foods a breeze. On the downside, they score easily even with light knife cuts and tend to warp after a couple of runs through the dishwasher. If you do use them, park the mats on top of your regular cutting board, which puts a little "give" under the knife. If you are using the mats instead of a cutting board, be aware that hard countertops, even with a mat on top, will readily roll the edges of softer knives. The mats are also easier to cut through when used on a hard surface. If you think of them as long-term disposables, these flexible cutting mats can be handy. Just throw them out as soon as they become scratched and sliced—about six to nine months in my kitchen. My favorites have a nonskid backing that keeps them from sliding around under the knife.

KNIFE STORAGE AND TRANSPORT

In between feats of culinary magic, you've got to put your knives somewhere. Storing them loose in a drawer is a serious no-no. The edges get dulled and damaged, and more important, *you* might get damaged when you stick your hand into the drawer. Lopping off a finger is not a suave and debonair way to impress your dinner date. There are several good storage options available. Which one you choose depends on your knives, your counter space, and your desire to show off. There seem to be two militant camps when it comes to knife storage, the Introverts and the Extroverts (or Innies and Outies, if you prefer). Extroverts value immediate accessibility and the chance to display their knives. They go for knife blocks and magnetic racks. Introverts are more interested in keeping their countertops clear of clutter. They are perfect candidates for in-drawer storage systems.

For the Extroverts, the slanted knife block is often an ideal solution. The first thing to realize is that you don't have to buy a set of knives just to get a block. Knife blocks are available—solo—in a variety of sizes and configurations. Buying your block separately from your knives allows you to better match your counter space and collection. It also allows you to save an empty slot or two for knives you might buy in the future. There are a couple of things to keep in mind when shopping for the ideal block. Make sure that it will accommodate your longest and widest knives. Many 10-inch chef's knives, for example, are 2 inches wide at the heel. You need at least one slot, preferably two, at least that wide so you have room when a sexy new chef's knife catches your eye. Make sure the block is tall enough. Many are open at the back, meaning the slots go all the way through. A block that is too short will allow the tip of your longest knife to poke through the back, putting little holes in your countertop and possibly damaging the tip of your knife. Even if your knife doesn't hit the countertop, it may still stick out of the back a little. Not a good thing if your cats hop up on the counter every once in a while. Don't think, though, that a closed-back block is a better idea. It isn't. You want air to be able to flow through the slots. You should always dry your knives before putting them away, but just in case, an open-back block will keep any moisture (and attendant bacteria) from accumulating.

Knife blocks come in vertical and horizontal slot configurations, meaning that your knives are either stored with the edge down or they are stored flat on their sides. Either way is fine. I have seen the argument that vertical slots can damage the edges of your knives but I don't buy it. A good wooden block is very much like a cutting board. An extra stroke on the edge here and there isn't going to do any harm to your edge. I suppose you might, over a very long time, wear a groove in the vertical slots. Just make sure that you have a slot for a honing rod (high-grit ceramic, please) and a good set of kitchen shears. Other than that, it's simply a matter of preference. There is even a style of block available that is filled with hundreds of thin plastic rods, eliminating the need for slots altogether. Simply slide your knife in wherever there is room and the rods clamp it in place. Nifty if you have shorter knives. Ten-inch and 12-inch knives stick out too far, leaving the heel and part of the cutting edge exposed.

Another option for the Extrovert is a magnetic knife rack. These strips mount on a wall or backsplash, freeing up counter space and drawer space. They are perfectly safe, but all of those exposed edges can be intimidating to non–knife fans. A magnetic bar also might not be your best bet if you have inquisitive children or pets. There is a technique to using a magnetic rack. You must roll the knife off and on the strip to avoid damaging the edge. Just place the spine of the knife on the rack first and rotate the blade down until it snaps into place. To remove a knife, reverse the process. Grasp the handle of the knife and using the spine as the fulcrum, rotate the blade off the magnets. That keeps you from scraping or grinding the edge of your knife on the bars.

Introverts also have a couple of fine options. One is a flat knife block that mounts to the underside of your kitchen cabinet. This style of block swivels the knife handles out of the way when you are not using them. Magnetic strips in the knife slots keep the knives from flinging out if you swivel the block too exuberantly. The only drawback is that you have to mount the block to your cabinets yourself. If you are the handy type, this style of knife block is a great way to free up counter space. For those of us who should be kept away from power tools at all costs, in-drawer knife trays are the best storage option. Unlike silverware trays, in-drawer knife trays have individual slots for each knife, larger slots for larger knives and smaller slots for paring knives or steak knives. Most of these trays look like flat boxes with slots cut in them and have a slanted area at the back where your knife handles rest. Boring. The absolute best in-drawer system around is the Wave from J. K. Adams Company (they also make great knife blocks). The Wave is sleek, sexy, and holds six large knives, eight smaller knives, and your honing rod in a two-tiered Art Deco–inspired tray. There is a smaller version that holds five chef's knives and six smaller knives. The Wave is the only in-drawer knife tray I've found that can accommodate a 12-inch knife. The only limitation to in-drawer trays is the depth of your drawers. A drawer that is too shallow won't close if there are tall handles in the tray.

The wave knife tray from J. K. Adams.

If you just have a knife or two and don't want to spring for a full block or in-drawer tray, you can always use sheaths or edge protectors. These range from simple slip-on plastic edge guards to elaborate knife safes, which are clamshell-type enclosures that snap firmly around your knife. Knife safes have rubber bumpers inside to keep the knife suspended away from the plastic. Some traditional Japanese knives even come with their own wooden sheath, called a *saya*. There are also folding magnetic strips that wrap around your knife to keep the edge (and your hands) safe. None of these sheaths is perfect. Knife safes are bulky and take up a lot of room. Plastic edge guards can trap grit and scratch the sides of you knife if you don't clean and dry your knife before putting it in the sheath. Magnetic edge guards can trap moisture and lead to

rust spots. In a pinch, you can create a makeshift sheath from a folded piece of cardboard taped closed with heavy packing tape. Despite their drawbacks, all of these options are better than putting your knives in a drawer unprotected.

Sheaths or edge guards come in handy when you need to transport your knives. Even if you have a professional folding knife roll, you should still protect your edges with some sort of sheath or guard inside the roll. Knife kits or knife rolls are made of heavy canvas or nylon and have elastic slots for your knives, kitchen tools, and honing steel. They generally have a shoulder strap for hands-free carrying. Knife rolls are rarely seen outside of culinary schools or professional kitchens, but for about $20 they are a great way to carry your knives if you do a lot of cooking away from home. For the truly hard core, there is even a culinary toolbox with a knife tray in the bottom. A second tray fits on top for spatulas, thermometers, or whatever other kitchen tools you might need.

Part Two
CUT LOOSE

5

ESSENTIAL KNIFE SKILLS

Now for the fun part. We finally put our knives to work. In this section we'll learn that the Pinch and the Claw, despite sounding like '60s dance crazes (or a really bad first date) are the keys to making precision cuts with speed, safety, and style. We'll also learn what some of those menu terms like *brunoise* and *batonnet* mean, and how (and why) to do them at home. Most important, you'll learn not to be intimidated by your knives or any presumed lack of skill. Most of the fancy French knife cuts follow the same basic steps. If you can stack children's building blocks, you can turn out restaurant-quality dice, julienne, or brunoise with just a little practice. To help you build your knife skills without mindlessly slicing up pounds of carrots or potatoes, try the "Knife Skills Workouts" on page 112. These will help you build speed and confidence while turning out dinner.

WHY BOTHER?

Why go to all the trouble to learn to cut perfect batonnet or to dice a carrot? In large part because it looks nice. Well-cut vegetables make for an eye-catching presentation. It shows the people you are cooking for that you care about the food and their enjoyment of it. In more practical terms, keeping your cuts uniform ensures that the food cooks evenly. You get the best flavor and texture from items that are cut to the same size and length. They all finish cooking at the same time and have the same texture. No mushy bits or hard, undercooked chunks.

> **Your knife, more than any other piece of equipment in the kitchen, is an extension of the self, an expression of your skills, ability, experience, dreams and desires.**
>
> —TONY BOURDAIN, *Les Halles Cookbook*

KNIFE SAFETY AND ETIQUETTE

Remember how you were taught to carry scissors in first grade? Point down and with the scissors by your side? Well, that's exactly how you carry a knife across the kitchen: tip down with the knife at your side, edge facing behind you.

If you need to hand a knife to someone else, there are two safe ways to go about it. The safest and easiest approach is to lay the knife down on the cutting board or countertop and let the other person pick it up. This is even safer if you rotate the handle toward the other person as you lay the knife down. That keeps them from reaching across the blade to grasp the handle. If laying the knife down isn't an option, flip the knife over and grasp the spine of the knife between your thumb and forefinger just above the handle. Tuck your other fingers into your palm. Present the knife to the other person handle first. Holding the knife by the spine keeps the edge away from your fingers. Even if the other person suffers a moment of tragic thoughtlessness (or even a sneezing fit) and tugs the knife out of your hands, all of your precious pink digits stay safe.

> **If you cut yourself, you are going too fast or you are not focused.**
>
> —SARA MOULTON, Executive Chef, *Gourmet* magazine, author of *Sara's Secrets for Weeknight Meals*

One last safety precaution: Imagine one of those zip line key rings that every school janitor seems to own. You know, the kind with a spring-loaded metal cable that pulls the keys back to his belt when he is finished with them. Now imagine an invisible zip line connecting your knife and your cutting board, pulling your knife down to the board whenever you are not actively cutting something. If you are finished with your carrots and need something from the fridge, zip, the knife goes down on the board. Just lay the knife flat on the cutting board and make sure that neither the tip nor the edge is hanging over the side of the board, and *then* go do whatever you need to do. Phone ringing? Zip, down on the board. Kid needs a Band-Aid and a hug? Zip, down on the board. Do not do anything with a knife in your hand but cut food. It doesn't matter if your cat is on the counter (again) or your dog has discovered the tasty chicken carcass in the garbage can (again)—whatever the emergency, lay the knife down first, preferably with the edge facing the back of the board. This alone will prevent a lot of kitchen accidents.

STABILIZE AND ORGANIZE

When you are ready to set up your cutting board, take a second or two to think about what foods you are preparing. Remember, you should have at least two cutting boards on hand if you are going to be cutting fruits or vegetables along with raw proteins. At the very least, do your slicing and dicing in order of final cooking temperature. Fruits and vegetables first. Raw meat and chicken gets prepped *last*.

Stabilize your cutting board by putting a damp towel or bit of shelf liner underneath to gain some traction. Even a damp paper towel will work. You don't want your board slipping around if you have to bear down with your knife. Not safe. Have a clean dishrag or paper towel handy for wiping the board down between items or to remove excess trim.

KITCHEN FIRST AID

If you pay attention to what you are doing, especially the position of your guide hand, you should not be afraid of cutting yourself. If it does happen, rinse the cut with mild soap and running water. You should have a basic first-aid kit in your kitchen stocked with sterile gauze pads, adhesive bandages, and antibiotic ointment. Blot the cut dry with sterile gauze or a clean cloth. Apply pressure with the gauze to stop any bleeding. It helps to raise the cut finger or hand above the level of your heart. Once the bleeding has stopped, apply antibiotic ointment and cover the wound with an adhesive bandage. The 3M Nexcare line of waterproof bandages is especially well suited for kitchen use. Unlike most bandages that claim to be waterproof but don't hold up in extended kitchen use, the Nexcare bandages stay on even with repeated hand washings or after scrubbing a sink full of dishes. Finger cots, which resemble small condoms for your fingers, can help protect cuts from moisture and can be used to cover a nonwaterproof bandage so you can keep working in the kitchen. They are available in most drugstores.

Any cut that bleeds profusely, appears deep or torn, is embedded with glass or debris, or causes any loss of feeling or mobility should receive professional attention at an emergency room or urgent care facility. ▲

Have a couple of bowls or containers handy: one for trim and one for the cut food. This will keep you from having to scoop carrot peels or broccoli stems into the garbage can every couple of minutes.

Try to work in one direction. It will save you a lot of time and effort. If you are right-handed, try working clockwise: uncut food on the left, refuse/trim bowl at the top of the cutting board at the twelve o'clock position, and a container for the finished, beautifully cut items on the right. Setting up a work flow like this isn't necessary if you are simply slicing a few strawberries for a bowl of ice cream, but if you are making minestrone, for example, where you have multiple ingredients to prepare, things will go much faster if you stay organized and follow a consistent pattern.

CLAW YOUR WAY TO THE TOP

Do not worry about going fast. You don't have an audience to impress. Speed comes from repetition. Learning to use your knife well is exactly like learning to type. Start off slowly and concentrate on precision rather than speed. The more practice you get, the faster you will get. And just like typing, proper hand position is important. That's why we need the Claw (cue scary music).

The Claw allows you to keep your knife moving without putting your fingers at risk. Your thumb is the anchor and stays safely tucked away in the cage of your fingers.

The Claw, more prosaically known as your guide hand, is the secret to getting your knife up to speed without fear of lopping off a finger. Place the tips of your fingers of your non–knife hand on the item to be cut. When you press down, your fingers will bend at the joint near the tips, folding your fingertips under a little. The front of your fingers between the first and second joints will be straight up and down. Move your thumb around behind your fingers. It is your anchor. As you slice you will glide your bent fingertips backward across the food, using your thumb to pull them. The knife rides up and down on the flats of your middle two knuckles. Your thumb is safely tucked away behind the cage of your fingers. If you see a TV chef looking directly into the camera while his or her knife blazes away, seemingly on its own, this is how it is done. Keeping the knife and guide hand in constant contact ensures that you know exactly where your edge and your fingers are at all times. It takes practice, though. At first it will be hard to keep your thumb from drifting out to the side to help grip whatever it is that you are cutting. As long as you keep your fingers bent with the tips tucked under and your thumb behind them, you can chop or slice quickly and safely. The distance you move your fingers back with each stroke determines how thick the slice will be. When your fingertips move all the way back to your thumb, pause for a moment to relocate your thumb farther back and start slicing again. Nothing to it.

The Claw allows you to chop or slice very quickly and very safely.

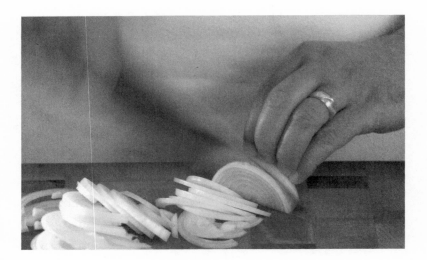

This does take practice. If you have an edge guard or sheath, slide it over your blade, put your hand in Claw position, lay the flat of the blade (safely encased in its plastic sheath) against your knuckles, and take a few practice slices. Remind yourself to keep your thumb tucked behind your fingers as you glide your bent fingertips backward. Move the knife with your fingers. You can do this on a cutting board or even on the countertop. The edge guard makes it easy to build the motions into muscle memory without fear of cutting yourself or the countertop.

PINCH ME

The Claw is your guide hand. The Pinch is your knife hand. More accurately, it is the way you hold your knife. The two work together in a symbiotic relationship. The Pinch is the yin to the Claw's yang. The Claw allows for precision cutting at speed. The Pinch is how you actually make those precise cuts. In the Pinch grip, the blade is grasped between your forefinger and thumb with your other three fingers loosely curled around the handle. To get the proper Pinch, hold the knife so that your first finger is flat against the blade just ahead of the bolster or collar. Your thumb should be on the opposite side of the blade, directly across from the second joint of your index finger. Your fingertip should naturally curl back so that it is clear of the heel. If you are used to gripping your knife by the handle like a fishing pole, the Pinch grip may seem a little uncomfortable at first. The Pinch has two major advantages that make it worth using. It aligns the knife with your wrist and forearm, which gives you added leverage and reduces fatigue, and it stabilizes the knife so that it cannot rotate in your hand. This not only keeps your cuts nice and straight but, more important, keeps the knife from twisting dangerously in your grip if you hit a bone or if a carrot wobbles while you are cutting.

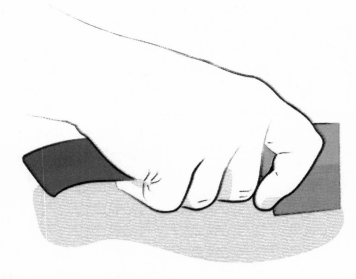

The Pinch gives you more control over the knife and prevents it from twisting in your hand.

LOOK WHERE YOU'RE GOING

When you've got the Pinch and Claw working and are ready to start cutting, stand square to your cutting board. When you stand naturally, your knife hand should point toward the opposite far corner, your guide hand the other far corner, forming an X right in front of your belly button. Now look down. What do you see? Probably the backs of your knuckles and the spine of your knife. Can you see *in front of* the knife? You should. That's where you are cutting. One of the most common mistakes is to look at the back of the knife. That's where your fingers are, so it's natural to keep an eye on that spot. What you want to see, however, is the cut you are currently making. You need to scoot your hands over just a little so that when you look straight down you are looking down the front side of the knife at the item being cut. That's the only way to know if your cuts are the proper thickness. Your fingers are safely out of the way. The Claw will see to that.

ROCK OUT!

How you slice depends on what you are cutting. For many foods, you can leave the tip of the knife on the board and rock the edge of the knife forward and down to slice through the food. Rock backward and up to reset your knife for the next stroke. Keep the tip on the board and the flat of the knife in contact with your fingers. This rocking motion can create mounds of julienne in a hurry because it is continuous. The knife never really stops. Rocking is particularly well suited to German-style knives. Their rounded bellies make rocking the knife feel very natural. Until you have a lot of time at the cutting board, the rocking technique is not going to produce perfectly symmetrical slices. Your cuts will get more and more even with practice, but rocking is more about speed than precision. It is also difficult to do with taller items like big onions, jicama, squashes, or anything that would require you to lift your elbow inordinately high on the return stroke. If it feels like you are jamming your shoulder into your ear, you are lifting too high. Rocking is not the answer. For that there are the push cuts and draw cuts.

PUSH/PULL

For harder vegetables like carrots, potatoes, or beets, start with the tip* of the knife on the vegetable rather than the cutting board. The position is similar to rocking but the edge of the knife is more horizontal and parallel to the board. You don't have to lift your elbow as high. Slice forward and down, the knife becoming more horizontal as it progresses through the vegetable. Just about the whole front third of the edge should be in contact with the cutting board at the bottom of the stroke. Follow through just a little farther to ensure that you've cut all the way through the food. Nothing is more frustrating than to have a dozen perfect slices still connected at the back corner because you stopped too soon and didn't slice all the way through. Slide your fingers and knife back

*It doesn't have to be the very tippy tip. The first inch or so of the edge is fine.

the correct distance for the next cut and make another slice. Because you reposition your knife on the vegetable each time you have more control and can produce more even cuts.

Follow through by gliding the knife forward to ensure that you've cut all the way through the item.

Want to try it backward? On softer fruits and vegetables where you have to puncture a skin that is tougher than the pulp inside (such as a tomato or plum), it is often easier to draw the knife through than to push it. Use the tip of the knife to slice down into the food and then pull the tip and edge back through the item. This is also an excellent way to make vertical cuts through an onion, shallot, or garlic clove. To butterfly pork chops or chicken breasts or to slice fish into portions, use the same draw cut but start at the heel of the knife. That gives you a long, smooth pull without having to saw through the food.

KNIFE SKILLS WORKOUTS

There is no reason to cut up a couple of pounds of vegetables just for the practice. You should at least get dinner or a side dish out of the deal. The following recipes will give you a chance to put your knife skills to work.

Julienned Vegetables

TECHNIQUE: Julienne

*Julienned vegetables make for a stylish side dish. They are
bright and colorful and add a professional touch to the plate.
The technique is so adaptable that you can use just about any
vegetables you like. Cut each vegetable into 2- to 3-inch lengths
before cutting planks and julienne. A basic combo that goes with
anything includes:*

2 medium carrots, julienned into ⅛-inch strips
(½ cup)

1 medium leek, julienned into ⅛-inch strips (½ cup)

2 large ribs celery, julienned into ⅛-inch strips
(½ cup)

Butter and olive oil, for sautéing

Technically, you should first blanch the vegetables in salted
boiling water for 20 to 30 seconds, then shock them in ice
water. That sets the color and allows you to hold them in the
fridge until you are ready to reheat them in a sauté pan with
a little butter. In practice you can just sauté them with butter
and olive oil over medium-high heat for 3 to 5 minutes, or
until they are tender. Use just enough butter and oil to lightly
coat the bottom of the pan. Remember, sauté means "to jump,"
so keep the veggies moving in the pan so they don't stick or
burn. If you like your vegetables very tender, you can give
them a quick sauté to develop the flavor, then add a little water or stock (less than ¼ cup) to the hot pan and cover. This
will steam the vegetables to your desired tenderness.

For added color, substitute one julienned red pepper for
the celery. You can also add julienned snow peas, zucchini,
squash, beets, or almost anything you like. Mix and match.
Harder vegetables take a little longer to cook, so add them to

the pan first to give them a head start before adding the softer vegetables. Julienned vegetables make a great bed for fish or chicken and look pretty snazzy as a garnish for thicker soups. You can even skip the sauté step and simply blanch the vegetables for about 1 minute to soften a little, and dress them with a light vinaigrette.

Summer Lentil Salad

TECHNIQUES: Small dice, chiffonade, mince

MAKES 4 servings as a light entrée

COOKING TIME: 30 to 40 minutes, plus 30 minutes
chilling

1 large tomato, seeded but not necessarily peeled
(see Tomatoes, Color Plates 26–27), cut into small
dice (¼-inch cubes)

1 medium cucumber, peeled and seeded, cut into small
dice (¼-inch cubes)

2 medium carrots, cut into small dice (¼-inch cubes)

1 large garlic clove, peeled and lightly crushed

½ quartered yellow onion (optional)

1 cup small green lentils, preferably French *lentilles
du Puy*

2 tablespoons sherry vinegar or cider vinegar, or to
taste

1 large shallot, finely diced or minced

¼ teaspoon freshly ground black pepper

1 tablespoon Dijon mustard

6 tablespoons extra virgin olive oil

¼ cup thinly sliced (chiffonade) fresh basil

2 tablespoons minced parsley (optional)

1 teaspoon salt or 2 teaspoons kosher salt

Dash of hot sauce (optional)

Mixed baby greens, for serving

Prep and set aside the tomato, cucumber, and carrots.

Add the garlic and onion, if using, to a pot with the lentils and cook the lentils according to the package directions. If the directions are unclear, start the lentils in about 3 cups cold water. Bring to a soft boil, reduce the heat, and cover. Simmer for 25 to 30 minutes, or until the lentils are cooked through but still hold a firm shape. Strain off excess liquid, remove the onion and garlic, and allow the lentils to cool to lukewarm.

In the meantime, combine the vinegar, shallots, pepper, and mustard in a mixing bowl. Whisk in the oil to create a basic vinaigrette. Gently fold in the lentils while still warm and allow to cool to room temperature. Add the tomatoes, cucumber, carrots, basil, and parsley, if using. Season with salt and pepper. I add a splash or two of Cajun hot sauce just to keep things interesting. Cover and chill 30 minutes to an hour. Serve over mixed baby greens.

For a more elaborate presentation, spoon the lentil salad into a lightly oiled ring mold (I use a 2-inch biscuit cutter). Pack lightly so the salad retains its round shape. Remove the mold and top the salad with a disk of goat cheese, or feta crumbles.

This same lentil salad can be made into a warm, hearty winter meal by substituting diced roasted beets or butternut squash for the tomato, basil, and cucumber. The beets add an earthy sweetness to the dish. You can add another dimension with diced fennel. Combine the dressing and the lentils while still warm, add the beets and fennel, if using, fold gently, and serve immediately.

Potato Leek Soup

TECHNIQUES: Medium dice, small dice, finely sliced leeks, brunoise

> **MAKES** about 2 quarts, enough for 8 servings (or 4 with plenty left over for freezing)
>
> **COOKING TIME:** about 45 minutes

This soup can be either rustic or refined. Without the cream and left chunky, it is a hearty midwinter family dinner. When pureed with the cream and topped with a bright garnish, you have a more elegant version suitable for brown-nosing your boss or the head of the homeowners' association who thinks your planned outbuilding/roller disco rink might not pass muster.

This soup also makes a great base for other variations. You can add carrots, broccoli, spinach, or parsnips. If adding hard vegetables, dice them small and add them to the simmering stock with the potatoes. Simmer until tender. Puree or not as you see fit.

2 tablespoons olive or canola oil

¼ pound thick-cut smoked bacon, cut into small dice (¼-inch cubes)

3 medium leeks, trimmed, rinsed, and cut across the grain into ⅛-inch strips (3 to 4 cups)

½ large yellow onion, cut into small dice, ¼-inch cubes (1 to 1½ cups)

6 cups chicken stock (if you don't have homemade stock, the Swanson reduced-sodium stuff is pretty good for store-bought)

4 medium or 3 large russet potatoes (1½ to 2 pounds), peeled and cut into medium dice, ½-inch cubes (about 4 cups)

Salt and pepper

½   pint (1 cup) heavy cream (optional)

Brunoise red pepper (fine-diced to ⅛-inch cubes), thinly sliced chives, minced parsley, or croutons, for optional garnish

Heat the oil in a heavy-bottomed saucepan or soup pot until it shimmers. Before the oil begins to smoke, stir in the bacon and sauté over medium heat for 5 to 7 minutes to render the fat. If the bacon starts to crisp too much, turn the heat down. There is still some additional cooking to do before we add any liquid, and even though the vegetables will help we don't want the bacon to turn into little carbon briquettes.

Add the leeks and onion and cook, stirring occasionally, for 10 to 15 minutes, until they are very soft and the leeks have reduced in volume by about half.

Add the chicken stock and potatoes, and season with salt and pepper. Use white pepper if you want to maintain the sophisticated pale vichyssoise look. Bring the soup to a boil, reduce the heat, and simmer for about 20 minutes, or until the potatoes are tender enough to fall apart.

The soup can be served as is or you can use a potato masher to break up the potatoes for the rustic version. I take it off the heat, add the cream, and puree with a stick (immersion) blender until mostly smooth. You can use a regular blender, too. Just be careful and work in batches. Garnish with any of the options listed above or simply top with buttery croutons.

TIPS, TRICKS, AND TECHNIQUES

1.   Partially freeze your bacon. Place your bacon in the freezer for about thirty minutes before you begin your prep work. It should be firm but not frozen solid. Once the bacon is firm, cut lengthwise into ¼-inch strips and then crosswise into ¼-inch cubes.

BASIC KNIFE SKILLS DEMONSTRATED!

THE PINCH AND THE CLAW

Don't push. Relax. Let the knife do the work for you. Learn to use the knife *strategically*.

—SARA MOULTON,

Executive Chef,

Gourmet magazine,

author of *Sara's Secrets*

for Weeknight Meals

For a proper Pinch grip, curl your forefinger flat along the side of the blade. Your thumb should be on the other side, almost directly opposite your second knuckle.

To keep your guide hand safe while keeping the item you are cutting as stable as possible, press down with your fingertips so they bend at the first knuckle.

Slide your thumb around behind the cage of your fingers. The thumb anchors your hand and pulls your fingers backward across the food as you slice. Your knife rests against the flats of your knuckles, gliding up and down as you cut.

When using a Chinese cleaver, the Pinch grip is even more vital. Even thin vegetable cleavers are very blade heavy. Most of your gripping strength and control will come from your thumb and forefinger. You don't have to curl your finger out of the way of the heel, so you have an even more stable grip.

Chinese cleavers are so tall that it is nearly impossible to raise the edge higher than your knuckles, making the Chinese cleaver very safe to use with proper technique.

PLANKS, LOGS, CUBES

The most precise cuts in the kitchen all follow the same four steps: squaring up, cutting planks, cutting logs, and cutting cubes. That's it. That's all there is to it. You can make these cuts to exact shapes and sizes for a more formal presentation, or more relaxed for an informal or rustic presentation. Let's take a look in detail.

Get Square—Vegetables and fruits, sadly, do not grow in square shapes. They are distressingly rounded. Even if you are just roughly chopping something for a stock or stew, you should slice or trim at least one side of a round food so that it sits flat on the cutting board. That gives you more control and makes cutting safer. If you are attempting classic precision cuts such as julienne or dice, square the food off by cutting slices from the top, bottom, and both sides so that you have a more rectangular shape to work with. Make your first cut and rotate the food over onto the flat side for the second cut. Rotate over onto the newly cut side for the third and so on.

Walk the Plank—The next step is to cut your newly rectangular food lengthwise into regular planks or panels. They should all be the same thickness. The width of the plank is determined by the final cut you are trying to achieve and its cooking time. Smaller cuts and faster cooking times mean thinner planks. Bigger cuts or longer cooking times mean thicker planks. Just make sure they are all the same size.

Log In—Stack the planks two or three high (depending on their thickness and slipperiness) and cut them lengthwise into logs that are the same width as the planks. Again the width is determined by the final cut.

Roll the Dice—Last, cut across the logs to produce dice. If you cut the planks, logs, and dice to the same width, you should end up with a neat cube that is the same size all the way around.

For the specifics on precision cuts, let's follow the story of those star-crossed lovers Batonnet and Julienne.

3

PRECISE CUTS

BATONNET AND JULIENNE

You can still hear them calling to each other across the Pont Neuf*, the sturdy, taciturn Batonnet and the slender, elegant Julienne, professing their undying yet impossible love.

Ah, young love. Alas. Even though not a classic tragic love story, *batonnet* (ba-taw-NAY) and *julienne* (joo-lee-EHN) are classic precision knife cuts. They follow the pattern of squaring up, cutting planks, and cutting logs, but differ in final size. Notice that the "cube" step is missing. Batonnet and julienne stop at the log or stick stage and generally are served as side dishes. Each has a corresponding dice size.

For batonnet, square off the vegetable and cut planks ¼ inch (6 mm) thick. Cut the planks into logs ¼ inch (6 mm) wide. Those are not absolute measurements. You don't have to check each batonnet with a ruler when you are making dinner. As long as each cut is about the right size and, more important, the same size as the others, everything will be fine. If you've ever cut carrot sticks for your child's lunch box, you've cut batonnet. This is also the basis for the standard french-fry cut, though fries are a little thicker, around ⅓ to ½ inch.

---

* *Pont Neuf* or "New Bridge" is the name of a famous Parisian bridge built in 1607. It is also the name of a famous french-fry cut. We would call them steak fries. They are more rustic than a precise cut and don't require the potato to be obsessively squared off before starting.

CHEAT YOUR WAY TO BATONNET

Yeah, sure, you say. I'll just put on my bionic laser glasses that allow me to judge vegetable thickness to 1/64 inch. Relax. No laser vision needed. You can cheat. If you have a standard German or French chef's knife, the spine will usually be between ¼ and 1/8 inch just in front of the handle. A little more than halfway down the blade, right where your guide hand knuckles usually touch, the spine narrows to within a couple thousandths of an inch of 1/8. Perfect. That's your visual guide. For batonnet, simply move your Claw fingers back two spine widths (¼ inch). For julienne, move them back one spine width (1/8 inch) and slice away. If you have a modern Japanese-made knife, the spine will be thinner but still pretty close. Just slide your fingers back slightly more than a spine width for 1/8 inch.

 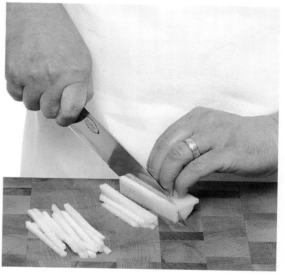

For julienne, cut planks ⅛ inch (3 mm) thick and cut those into ⅛ inch (3 mm) matchsticks. In fact, the French term for potatoes cut to this size is *allumette* or "matchstick." Both batonnet and julienne are usually cut into 2- to 3-inch lengths. The actual size depends on how the cuts are used. If you've julienned leeks for your vegetable soup, cut the lengths to fit inside your soup spoons so they don't hang over the sides and make eating difficult. If you have julienned a red pepper to sprinkle on top of a salad, the sticks can be the standard 2-inch length. Matchstick potatoes for shoestring fries can be as long as you like. With hard vegetables like carrots, it is easier to cut the food to length before squaring it off.

For the truly fanatical, there is also a fine julienne that is ¹⁄₁₆ by ¹⁄₁₆. This can be very tricky to cut by hand but makes for a spectacular presentation.

CUBISM

The last step in our four-step program is cutting cubes—dicing. Diced vegetables are used in soups and stews as side dishes and as garnishes. The size of the dice is determined by the size of the log or stick you cut in the previous step. When you cut across the logs, cut to the same width as the log to produce an even cube. Remember that one spine width is about ⅛ inch and two spine widths is about ¼ inch. That gives you a good visual reference for the distance to move your guide hand fingers and knife for each cut.

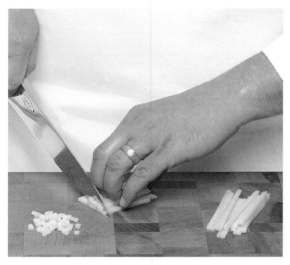

Julienne, when cut across into cubes, produces a fine dice called *brunoise* (broon–WAHZ) measuring ⅛ x ⅛ x ⅛ inch.

Cutting across a batonnet produces *small dice* (¼ x ¼ x ¼ inch).

The french-fry cut when cubed produces *medium dice* (½ x ½ x ½ inch).

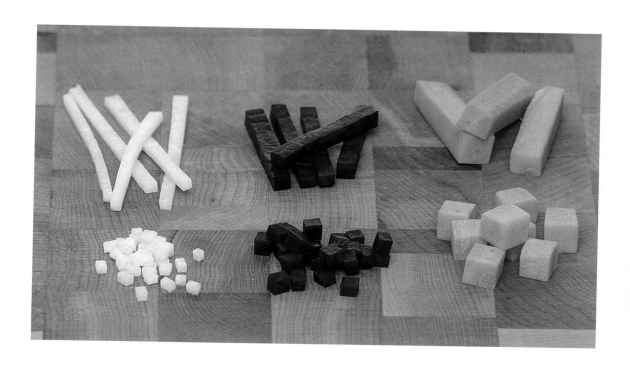

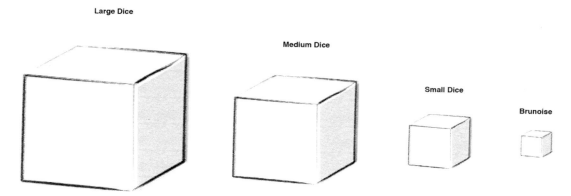

Large Dice

Medium Dice

Small Dice

Brunoise

Large dice measures ¾ x ¾ x ¾ inch, and is generally used only for hearty stews, roasted root vegetables, or chunky fruit salads.

There you go. Precision knife work made simple. It takes practice, but if you take your time you can turn out perfect *brunoise* with just a little effort.

INFORMAL AND RUSTIC CUTS

Maybe precision cuts aren't on the menu tonight. If you are not feeling quite so stylish or just don't want to work that hard, there are the informal or rustic cuts. These are bread-and-butter, everyday knife skills. You are probably already making some of these cuts; you just didn't know the proper name.

ROUGH CHOP

The most basic cut is a rough chop. The pieces are usually left large and are not as exact as a dice. They just have to be regular and approximately the same size. Carrots, onions, and celery for making stock and vegetables for hearty stews are good candidates for a rough chop, as is anything used as a flavoring that will eventually be strained out of the final dish.

Peel the vegetable and trim off the root and stem, if necessary.

Make consistent cuts across the item to cut it into pieces roughly the same size. They do not have to be perfectly even. Chop into larger pieces for long cooking, smaller pieces for shorter cooking times.

There are people who love to be in the kitchen, to immerse themselves in that experience. It's a Zen thing. A good knife can help facilitate that.

—BOB KRAMER,
ABS Master Bladesmith

SHREDDING

This cut is most often used for cabbage. Shredding can be done coarsely or finely, depending on the food's final use (or how hefty you like your coleslaw). Shredding works best for tightly packed heads. Loose-leafed veggies get the chiffonade treatment.

Cut the cabbage in half lengthwise.

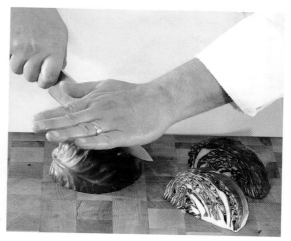

Cut each half lengthwise into quarters, cutting through the stalk.

Cut out the hard core.

Place a cabbage quarter cut side down on the board to keep it stable and cut across into shreds.

CHIFFONADE

Chiffonade (shif-ə-NAHD) is a finer and more regular form of shredding, used to slice leafy vegetables and greens into thin strips or ribbons.

Hearty greens like chard or kale need to have the center rib cut out first. Simply draw the tip of the knife down each side of the rib to separate it from the leaf and remove it. With tender leaves such as spinach or basil, the rib can be sliced along with the leaves.

 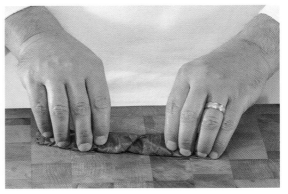

For larger leaves, roll the individual leaves into a tight cigar. Stack smaller leaves before rolling.

Cut across the cylinder to produce fine ribbons.

MINCING

When a recipe calls for you to mince something, it means to cut the food into very small pieces. As with the rough chop, exact size isn't as important as uniformity. You usually mince herbs, but the term is also used for very finely chopped onions or garlic (visit "The Alliums" starting on page 18). To mince slender members of the onion family such as scallions or chives, bunch them up and make very fine slices across.

For leafy herbs, gather them into a tight bunch on the board and slice across with your chef's knife.

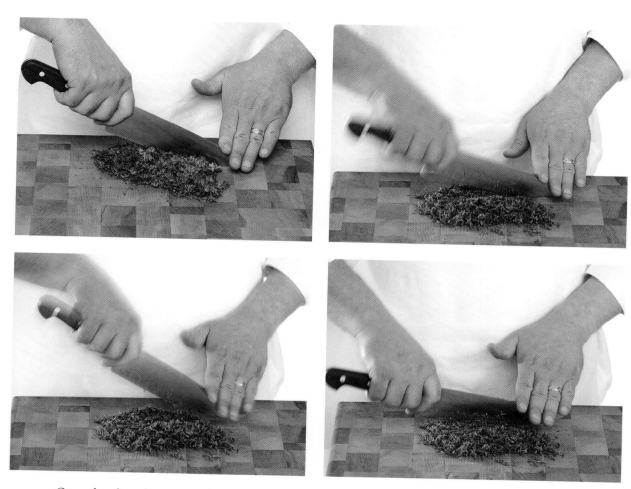

Once they have been coarsely cut, place the fingertips of your guide hand on the spine of the chef's knife near the tip and repeatedly rock the knife through the herbs, keeping the tip on the board, until you've reached the desired fineness. You may have to scrape the herbs back into a bunch as they are scattered by the chopping.

RONDELLES AND BIAS CUTS

Rondelles* (rahn-DELZ) or rounds are about as easy as it gets. Peel a carrot, parsnip, or other cylindrical vegetable and slice across at regular intervals. The thickness depends on your final use. You've probably done this hundreds of times. Now you know what it's officially called.

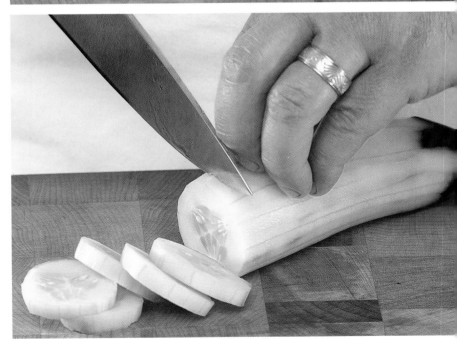

* I believe *Chiffonade and the Rondelles* would be the greatest doo-wop group name ever. Shoop shoop shooby do.

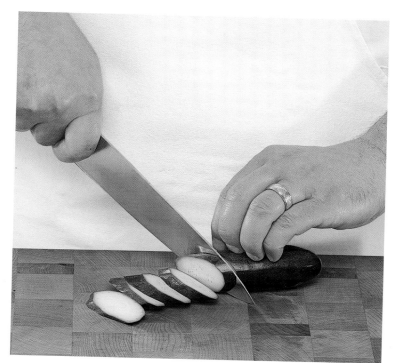

Show your bias! A bias cut is a diagonal slice across a vegetable. It is often used for fruits or vegetables that will be grilled or stir-fried because it exposes more surface area for faster cooking. Hold the knife at an angle to the vegetable and make regular slices across.

Bias-cut zucchini, shown here, is great when threaded onto skewers, brushed with olive oil, and grilled for 4 to 5 minutes until just tender.

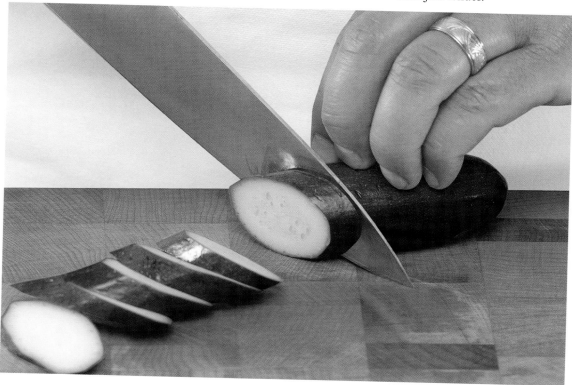

OBLIQUE (ROLL) CUT

Used for stir-fries or if you simply want a more interesting appearance, an oblique cut is essentially two bias cuts put together.

Slice diagonally across the vegetable at about a 45-degree angle. The flat side of the cut will face away from you.

Roll the vegetable toward you until the freshly cut side is facing you—a half rotation of the carrot—and cut across again at the same angle.

Roll it back for the next cut, creating little round-bottomed pyramid shapes. For more asymmetrical shapes, roll the vegetable a quarter turn each time rather than a half. This will give each cut an interesting faceted shape.

PAYSANNE

The *paysanne* (pay-ee-ZANN) or "peasant" cut is intended to be rustic and homey. Cuts produced in the paysanne style follow the natural contours of the vegetable, cutting it into ⅛- to ¼-inch slices.

It is still important that the pieces be the same size for even cooking and attractive presentation, but you don't have to obsess over squaring off the vegetable. Cut the vegetable into halves or quarters and slice across evenly. Here a carrot has been cut into quarters (lined up side by side to cut four at a time) and sliced ⅛ inch thick to create a nifty triangle shape.

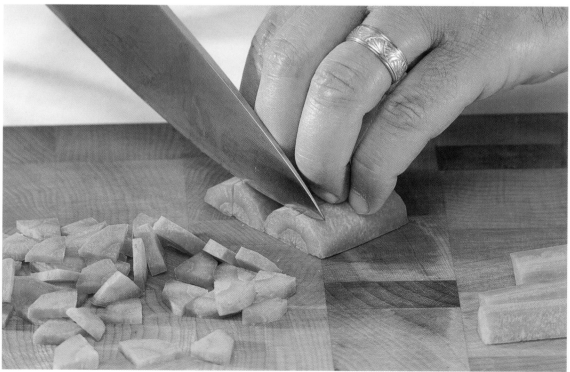

THE ALLIUMS: ONIONS, GARLIC, AND LEEKS

As far as I'm concerned, the allium family is proof that the universe is a magical place and that we are meant to be happy. Alliums include onions, shallots, garlic, leeks, scallions, and chives. It would be nearly impossible to cook without them. It certainly would be impossible to cook *well* without them. However, they also have some idiosyncrasies that make cutting them up a little trickier than other vegetables.

DICING AN ONION

An onion has a stem end, where the leaves come together at the top, and a root end, the beard-like area at the bottom. Slice the top of the onion (the stem end) off to create a flat side.

Turn the onion over onto the flat side and cut lengthwise in half from root to stem. Leave the root intact and peel the onion.

Lay one flat side down on the cutting board and make a series of three to five horizontal cuts, drawing the knife through from heel to tip in one smooth motion. Slice deeply, but do not cut through the root. It will hold everything together for you.

You can use your guide hand in Claw position to stabilize the onion or you can use the Flying Hand Trick and place your hand on top of the onion with your fingers and thumb stretched out and curled upward, just like flying your hand out the car window when you were a kid. That keeps your fingers safely out of the way and can be a little less intimidating than cutting toward your fingers.

Now make a series of evenly spaced parallel cuts lengthwise through the onion. Slice downward with the tip of the knife near the root of the onion and draw the blade backward. This down-and-back motion will keep the onion together better than simply pressing the knife down through the onion. Remember to leave the root intact.

Rotate the onion and cut across the vertical slices to produce an even dice. The number of horizontal and vertical cuts determines the fineness of the dice. The more cuts and the more closely spaced they are, the finer the dice. Fewer, wider slices produce a medium dice.

THE QUARTER-ROLL TRICK

If the idea of making horizontal slices—and cutting toward your hand—gives you the willies, there is always the Quarter-Roll Trick. This method is a little slower than the standard technique, but it is plenty fast for home use.

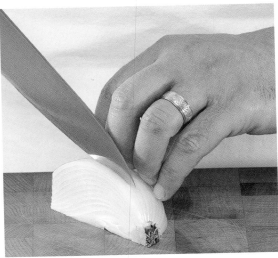 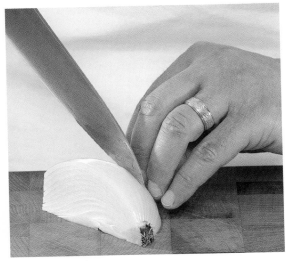

As before, cut off the stem end of the onion. Turn it over onto the flat side and cut the onion in half lengthwise and peel. Cut the halves into quarters lengthwise. Make a series of even vertical cuts lengthwise from root to stem, slicing down with the tip of the knife and drawing it back through the onion.

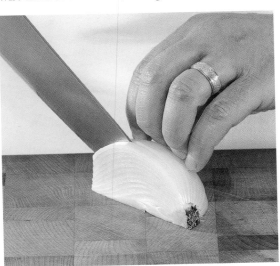 

Rotate the onion over onto the other flat side and do the same thing. Make a similar number of evenly spaced lengthwise slices. The first series of cuts, now that they have been rotated 90 degrees, become your horizontal slices. The second series of cuts become your vertical cuts.

We remember the fish, which we did eat in Egypt freely; the cucumbers, and the melons, and the leeks, and the onions, and the garlic.

—Numbers, 11:5

As before, cut across the onion to turn out an even dice.

NO MORE TEARS

Onions hold sulfur compounds in the liquids within the cell walls. When the cell is crushed or damaged, vacuoles containing an enzyme break open, allowing the enzyme to mix with the sulfur compounds and create a volatile compound that attacks the eyes and nose. It is this compound, the *lachrimator,* that causes our eyes to water and nose to run when we cut onions. You can do two things to limit how much lachrimator you have to deal with. First, use a very sharp knife. A keen edge will slice the cell walls rather than crushing them, limiting the amount of enzymes that get mixed in. Second, chill the onion in a bowl of ice water for half an hour to an hour before cutting. That slows the enzyme activity down considerably and reduces the volatile compounds.

SHALLOTS

Shallots look like the unholy love child of onions and garlic. Like onions, they grow in layers. Like garlic, they grow in cloves. You need some. Shallots are milder than onions but have a deeper and more complex flavor. They are the secret to a lot of restaurant food, especially sauces, vinaigrettes, and sautéed foods where onions would be harsh and overpowering.

The cloves of a shallot are joined at the base by the root, just like garlic. Because of the way the cloves grow together there will always be a flat side. Break apart the cloves and peel just as you would an onion. Lay the flat side down on your cutting board and dice the shallot like a small onion—start with a series of horizontal cuts, then vertical cuts, then across for a fine dice. This is one of the rare instances where a paring knife is preferable to a chef's knife.

GARLIC, GARLIC, GARLIC

Skip those rubber tube garlic peeler things. They are completely unnecessary and a pain to wash. As with 90 percent of everything else in the kitchen, all you need is a sturdy chef's knife to peel, chop, and mince garlic.

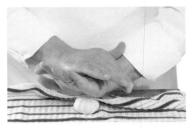

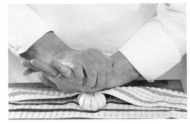

When you break a whole head of garlic into cloves, you can use a side towel to simplify cleanup of the papery skin. Lay the head of garlic on the towel and fold a flap of the towel over it.

Press down with the heel of your hand on the top of the garlic to break it into individual cloves.

Place individual cloves on the cutting board and lay your chef's knife flat on the clove. Press down with the heel of your hand to pop the skin free. Peel off the skin and remove the hard root end of the clove.

Lay the flat of your knife on the clove again and hit the blade firmly with the heel of your hand or the side of your fist to lightly crush it. If the clove has sprouted, split it open and re-move the green sprout, which can make the garlic taste bitter.

For an even mince, make a series of vertical cuts through the clove, then cut across.

To mince further, chop the garlic with a rocking motion just as you would for herbs, the fingers of your guide hand resting on the spine of the knife.

For an even finer mince, sprinkle coarse salt on the chopped garlic and press the knife nearly flat onto the garlic and scrape backward. The salt acts as an abrasive and keeps the garlic from sticking to the side of the knife.

Continue pressing and scraping until you have a thick paste.

The more finely garlic is chopped, the more pungent it becomes.

LEEKS

Like other members of the onion family, leeks grow in layers. Unlike other members of the family, they suck up a lot of sand and dirt. They are almost always sandy and gritty between the layers and usually have some soil trapped around the root.

Lay the rinsed leeks on your cutting board and remove the dark green tops.

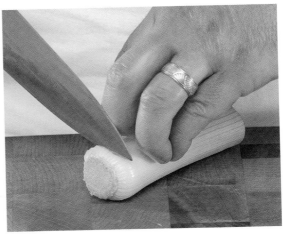

Cut the leek into 2- to 3-inch lengths.

Trim away the root end and slice the leek in half lengthwise.

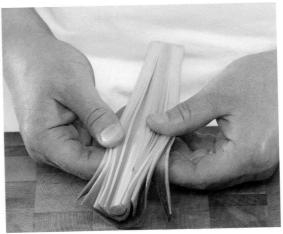

Fan it open like a book and rinse under running water to remove any sand or dirt.

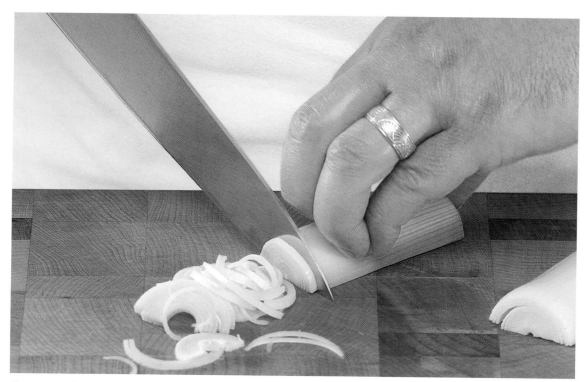

Cut across the leek to produce thin slices that will break down in cooking. This is especially helpful when making leek soup, where you want the leeks to almost dissolve into the soup.

Slice the leeks into julienne when you want them to hold together, as in a side dish of sautéed julienned vegetables.

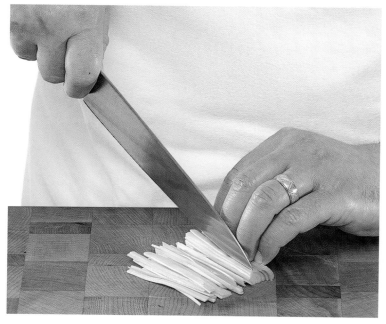

OTHER FRUITS AND VEGETABLES

Just as onions, garlic, shallots, and leeks have their own cutting techniques, other fruits and vegetables—especially those with tough outer skins and soft, pulpy interiors—can seem problematic until you know the tricks of the trade.

TOMATOES

While salad tomatoes are simply sliced or quartered, tomatoes for sauces, salsas, and side dishes are usually peeled and seeded. This prevents the sauce from becoming too watery or harboring tough bits of tomato peel.

Use the tip of a paring knife to cut around the core of the tomato. Pinch the knife between your thumb and forefinger near the tip. This turns the tip of the paring knife into a depth gauge that will prevent you from gouging too deeply into the tomato. Rotate the tomato around the tip of the knife and cut the core out.

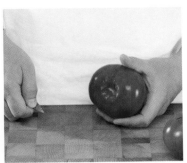

Score a small X in the skin at the base of the tomato, the blossom end. This will make it much easier to remove the skin.

Bring a large pot of water to a boil while you core and score the tomatoes. Have a bowl of ice water on hand as well.* Immerse the tomato in the boiling water for 20 to 30 seconds, or until the skin splits. If you have several tomatoes to prepare, drop two or three at a time into the water. Do not crowd the pot or the temperature of the water will drop below the boiling point and slow things down. Scoop the tomato out of the boiling water and submerge it in the ice water bath to prevent any further cooking.

---

* This method of blanching and peeling also works well with peaches, plums, and apricots.

Trap the split skin between your thumb and the flat of the paring knife and peel the skin away. It should come away easily in a thin layer.

Cut the tomato in half across the equator, not through the stem.

Gently squeeze the tomato and remove the seeds and jelly with your fingers.

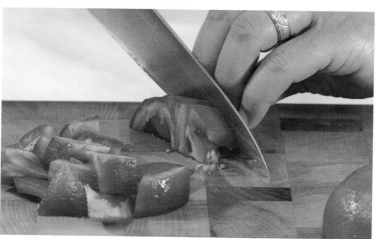

Lay the tomato cut side down on the cutting board and cut into strips. Cut across the strips for a rough dice called *concassé* (kawn-ka-SAY). For a finer dice, begin with a series of horizontal cuts just as you would with an onion.

PEPPERS

Peppers have a cluster of seeds attached to the stem end and the ribs. While you can simply quarter the pepper and remove the stem and seeds with a paring knife, this method is faster and allows you to produce a very neat julienne or dice. It also looks *really* cool when done smoothly. Practice on a pepper or two before showing off for your guests.

Slice off the top and bottom of the pepper (the stem and blossom ends) to remove the shoulders and narrower bottom.

Make a shallow slice just through the flesh of the pepper and rotate your knife so that it is flat and parallel to the cutting board, trapping the pepper between your knife and the board.

Place the palm of your guide hand on top of the pepper and roll the pepper open, following along with your knife to cut through the ribs in one smooth motion.

Keep the knife parallel to the pepper and the cutting board. You may not be able to roll out a whole pepper on your first try.

You will probably angle the knife down a little and cut through the pepper. Don't worry about it. Pause for a second, reset your knife where it needs to be, and keep going.

Cut the pepper into 2- to 3-inch panels and trim off any ribs or membrane that remains so the pepper is a uniform thickness.

Slice across the panels at $1/8$-inch intervals for a neat julienne.

MELONS

When serving slices or wedges of melon the rind is often left on. For diced melon in fruit salads or fruit plates, it is easier to remove the rind first.

Remove a slice from the bottom of the melon so that you have a stable surface on the cutting board.

Follow the curvature of the melon with your chef's knife to carve the rind away, taking as little of the melon flesh with the peel as possible.

Trim off any peel or rind that you might have missed.

Cut the melon in half and scoop out the seeds with a spoon. Lay the melon cut side down on the board and cut it into wedges.

Cut across the wedge for a rough dice. The size of the dice depends on the thickness of the wedge and the spacing between the cuts.

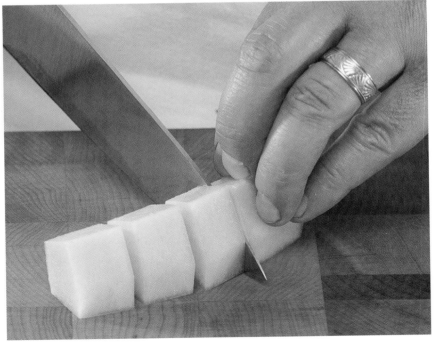

THE MEAT OF THE MATTER: PROTEINS*

We don't cut much meat at home anymore, which is a shame. We're not even buying whole chickens anymore, which is an even bigger shame. Everything comes prepackaged, parted out, portion controlled, sanitized, and completely unrecognizable as something that came from an animal. Next we will be lining up to have predigested protein mush fed to us via funnel on our way to work.

Emancipate yourself from boring chicken breasts. Buy a whole chicken. A basic roasted chicken is a fairly simple weeknight meal and the leftovers can be chopped and scattered on salads, made into quesadillas or potpies, or sliced for sandwiches. Cutting a whole chicken into pieces for grilling, baking, or frying isn't hard, either. And it's cheap. Those oh-so-convenient (and curiously flavorless) boneless skinless chicken breasts are *six or seven times* more expensive per pound than a whole bird. If you do cut up a chicken, save the carcass in the freezer to make stock.[†]

THE MICK JAGGER TRICK

If you have never cut up a chicken and are a little confused about how to tell the breast side from the backbone side, think of Mick Jagger. No, really. Imagine the iconic Mick Jagger strut—bent slightly at the waist, chest puffed out, elbows thrust around behind his back. Your chicken is in the same pose. Stand her up and sing "Honky Tonk Woman" and you'll see it immediately. If you are still not sure, the breast is rounded with a distinct ridge running down the center, while the back is flatter. The wings are attached at the back. The seam of the thigh is on the breast side. If you look in the neck cavity, the V of the wishbone points toward the breast side.

* Please note the separate cutting board used solely for raw meats.
[†] Stock is the easiest and tastiest kitchen cheat ever. I keep two large zip-top bags in the freezer, one for chicken parts and one for leek tops, carrot trimmings, leftover celery, and onions. Every couple of months they go into a large pot for an afternoon of stock making so that I always have a potent base for soups, gravies, or pan sauces on hand.

CUTTING UP A CHICKEN

There are two basic approaches to cutting a chicken into parts. The first method leaves you with boneless breasts. Take note that there is no need to hack through any bones. All cutting is *through* the joints, separating the ball from the socket.

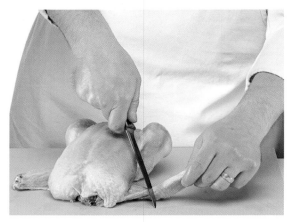

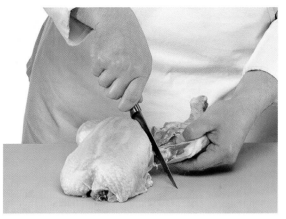

Remove the wing at the second joint. Bend the joint and cut through the skin so you can see where the two bones meet. Cut between them to remove the wing bone.

Cut down through the skin at the seam between the leg and the body. Bend the leg back (outward) to expose the joint. Keep bending until you hear or feel the ball of the thigh pop free from the socket.

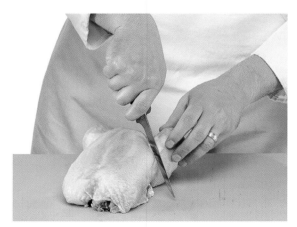

Cut between the ball and socket and around to the backbone. Roll the chicken over onto its side to make the last part of this cut easier. There is a choice nugget of meat called the oyster where the thigh meets the backbone that you don't want to

leave behind. Gently pull the thigh out and away from the carcass as you get near the tail and the oyster should come free from the hip joint. Repeat with the other leg.

Make a cut along one side of the breastbone or keel bone (that's the ridge running down the center of the breast).

Make light cuts with the tip of your knife to detach the breast meat from the bone as you pull the breast free with your guide hand or the flat of your knife.

Gently peel the breast away from the breastbone and rib cage, leaving as little meat on the bone as possible. Use the tip of your knife to cut through

any muscle fibers that don't want to let go. Remove the other breast and trim off any fat or loose skin.

To separate the thigh from the drumstick, flip the leg over. There is a white line of fat right at the joint where the two bones connect. Wiggle

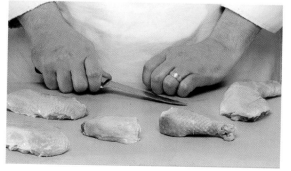

the drumstick so you can see the joint. Cut down through the fat line to cut the drumstick and thigh apart.

SPATCHCOCKING

Spatchcocking is the term for splitting a chicken or other bird down the back and spreading the halves flat for grilling or roasting. Besides making for a great table presentation, a spatchcocked bird takes less time to cook and cooks more evenly, keeping the meat moist. And it's fun to say.

In addition to allowing you to grill or roast the bird flat, this method is a quick and easy way to cut a chicken in half and from there into four, six, or eight pieces. As shown, this method leaves you with bone-in breasts.

You can spatchcock your bird with a chef's knife, but a pair of kitchen shears also works wonders. You will be cutting through rib bones, so more force is required than the previous method.

Turn the bird over so that it is breast side down on the cutting board. Cut along one side of the backbone, cutting through the ribs.

Cut along the other side of the backbone. The center strip containing the backbone will be ½ to ¾ inch wide.

Remove the backbone and open the chicken like a book.

Turn the chicken over and use the heel of your hand to press it flat. This ensures that the bird cooks evenly. It also helps loosen the keel bone.

Turn the chicken over again. In the center, between the breasts, is a line of white cartilage at the top of the keel bone. Slit the cartilage with your knife. If necessary, slide your fingers underneath the bird and fold the sides outward to expose the keel bone.

Grasp the keel bone and rotate it up and back to remove it and its attached cartilage from the breast. Trim away any loose fat or other unlovely bits. At this point you have a spatchcocked chicken ready to be marinated or patted down with a dry rub in preparation for the grill. A spatchcocked chicken also is much easier to season under the skin than a whole chicken.

If you cut down between the breasts you will have two chicken halves, each with a wing, breast, thigh, and leg (perfect for *pollo al mattone*—chicken under a brick, page 123). There is a natural crease between the thigh and the breast. Cut through that crease to create four pieces—two wing/breasts and two leg/thighs. Separate the leg from the thigh as in the first method for six pieces—two wing/breasts, two thighs, and two drumsticks. For eight pieces (and wings with a little meat on them), cut the wing free about two-thirds of the way down the breast.

You also have the option of removing the breast meat from the bone. Use the tip of your boning knife to separate the breast from the rib cage, working from the wing end to the thin end of the breast. For a classic breast presentation, trim away the wing at the second joint and scrape the meat from the remaining wing bone with the edge of your knife to expose the bone completely—almost like a little handle. This is called, without apparent irony, "frenching the bone." The breast may be sautéed or grilled.

BUTTERFLYING

Another basic skill that every cook should have in his or her repertoire is the ability to butterfly a pork chop, fillet, or chicken breast. To butterfly a cut of meat, you split it *almost* in half horizontally without separating the two halves, leaving a connected section in the center as a hinge. The cut opens up like a book (or a butterfly) for stuffing or pounding flat into a cutlet.

Butterflying violates one of the supposed tenets of knife handling: the rule that you never cut toward yourself. As we have seen with the horizontal cuts when dicing an onion, the rule can be broken safely if you know what you are doing with your guide hand. The Flying Hand Trick comes in handy here. You may also need to change your grip on the knife. When you slice horizontally, the standard Pinch grip sometimes does not give your hand enough clearance above the cutting board. To get your knife parallel to the board, keep your thumb on the flat of the blade so the knife cannot rotate, and move your forefinger to the top of the spine.

Place your knife in the middle of the thickest edge of the chop or breast with the knife parallel to the cutting board. Start the cut near the heel of the knife. Do not press down very hard with your

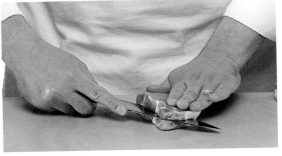

guide hand or you will make the cut more difficult. Your guide hand is there solely to keep the meat from slipping.

Draw the knife through the meat in one smooth sweep, cutting through almost to the far side but leaving about ¼ inch uncut at the back edge.

Fold the chop or breast open like a book. Using just the tip allows you to leave the meat together on three sides with a pouch for stuffing.

The same technique is used to butterfly shrimp. Use a paring knife to slice through the outer curve (back) of the shrimp and scrape out the "vein" (really the intestinal tract).

SKINNING SALMON, SNAPPER, OR OTHER FISH FILLETS

A fillet knife has a lot more flex to it than does a boning knife, even though they are sometimes used interchangeably. The flexibility of the fillet knife allows it to ride along the backbone and ribs of the fish without cutting through.

To skin a fillet, lay it on the cutting board with the smaller tail side nearest your guide hand. Make a small incision down through the fish to the skin about ½ inch from the end—enough room to ensure a good hold with your guide hand.

Turn the knife nearly flat against the skin. Hold the skin taut with your guide hand and angle the knife down slightly so the edge is cutting against (but not through) the skin.

Pull the skin with your guide hand while slicing forward with your knife in a smooth motion. There should be very little sawing.

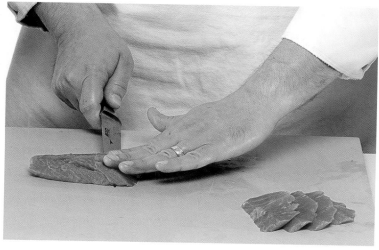

Cut the fish free from the skin, turn it over, and trim away any remaining skin.

Cut across the fillet at a slight bias to create smaller portions.

CARVING A TURKEY (OR CHICKEN OR DUCK)

The kerver must knowe the kervynge and the fayre handlynge of a knyfe and how ye shalle fesche all maner of fowle; your knife must be fayre and your handes must be clene.

—WYNKEN DE WORDE, *The Boke of Kervynge (Book of Carving),* 1508

One of the great secrets to roasting and carving meat is the resting period between the time the turkey, chicken, ham, or roast comes out of the oven and the time it is carved. As the internal temperature drops, the meat becomes firmer and, more important, its liquid-holding ability increases. Cut into it too soon and you end up with dry fibrous meat in a puddle of tasty liquid. Let it rest and you have tender, juicy slices of goodness that will ensure your place at the head of the table for years to come. A half-hour rest is usually about right, but larger or thicker cuts may take longer. If you have an instant-read thermometer, shoot for about 120°F (50°C) before slicing.

If you are smart, you'll carve your turkey, duck, or goose in the kitchen, away from prying eyes, and deliver a platter of sliced meat to the table. It is much faster and easier when no one is looking. There are two ways to go about it: family style and restaurant style.

Family style is the archetypal Norman Rockwell turkey carving, done at the table with slices presented to each diner as they are carved off the breast. Restaurant style is usually done in the kitchen. It doesn't have the drama of family style, but the slices are more uniform and hold their heat better.

Carving usually involves a slicing knife rather than a chef's knife. The long blade of a slicer allows you to make clean slices with a single stroke. The narrowness of the blade helps keep foods from sticking to it.

Start both family style and restaurant style by removing the wing by cutting through the second joint.

Remove the legs by cutting through the skin at the crease where the thigh joint meets the breast.

Pull the thigh away from the body to rotate the joint out and up. It will probably pop free. Cut through the joint and remove the thigh.

If carving family style, you can make a horizontal cut at the base of the breast to allow the slices to fall free cleanly at the bottom of the cut. Then slice the breast parallel to the rib cage using

long, smooth strokes. Do not saw. Pay attention to the wishbone at the neck end of the bird. It will interfere with your carving if you don't work around it.

To carve the bird restaurant style, remove the whole lobe of the breast. The ridge running along the center line of the turkey is its breastbone. Make a cut just to one side of the breastbone, keeping the knife as close to the bone as possible. Pull the breast away from the bone and continue making long, smooth slices right along the bone and rib cage to remove the breast intact.

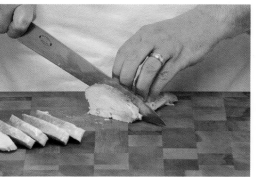 

Slice across the breast and arrange the slices on your serving platter. Thicker slices will retain their heat and juiciness longer than thin slices.

To carve the dark meat, hold the drumstick to keep the thigh steady and cut slices parallel to the bone. The leg and thigh can also be separated at the joint and carved separately.

STEELING AND SHARPENING

For more detailed instructions, see the sharpening section in Part Three.

STEELING

Steeling your knives regularly with a high-grit ceramic or smooth steel rod will keep your edges in top condition for months between sharpenings. The angle at which you steel is determined by the edge angle of your knives. If you have not yet sharpened your knives to a specific angle, assume that the factory edge is a little more than 20 degrees per side.

Use the Paper Airplane Trick (page 149) to set your angle or simply place the knife perpendicular to the steel to create a 90-degree angle.

Rotate the spine inward, cutting that angle in half to 45 degrees. Cut that angle in half again for 22.5 or so. It is important to keep the angle consistent as you stroke the edge down the steel. Lock your wrist and unhinge from the shoulder to keep the angle steady. Use a light touch, little more than the weight of the knife itself.

CLOCKWISE FROM TOP LEFT:
Knife Steeling High Left; Knife Steeling Mid Left;
Knife Steeling Lower Left

Knife Steeling High Right

Knife Steeling Mid Right

Knife Steeling Lower Right

SHARPENING WITH BENCHSTONES

Please note that the angles have been somewhat exaggerated to make the actions more clear in the photographs. When freehand sharpening without an edge guide, you would also have your free hand resting on the spine of the knife to help guide it.

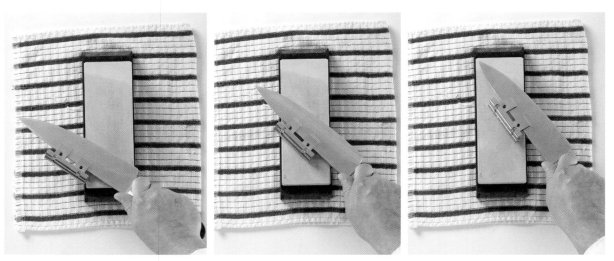

Place your stone on a damp towel so it doesn't slip. The basic stroke is from heel to tip with the edge moving into the stone.

The knife moves across the stone from one corner to the opposite corner. Here the knife is clamped into an edge guide to hold the edge at a consistent angle.

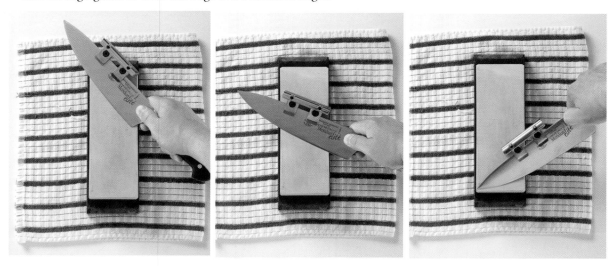

If sharpening freehand, place the fingertips of your other hand on the spine and flat of the knife to help keep the angle consistent. Lift the handle slightly at the end of the stroke to follow the curve of the edge up to the tip.

SHARPENING SYSTEMS

Crock sticks and V-systems allow you to simply hold the knife perpendicular to the tabletop and stroke down the length of the rod. Do not let the tip slide off the rod or you will round it over time.

Rod-style systems stroke the stone over the knife at a set angle. Some systems clamp onto the spine of the knife, which makes them difficult to use for large kitchen knives because you have to adjust the clamp as you move down the length of the knife. They are better for paring knives and pocket knives. The Edge Pro Apex allows you to slide the knife along the table to sharpen each section of the knife.

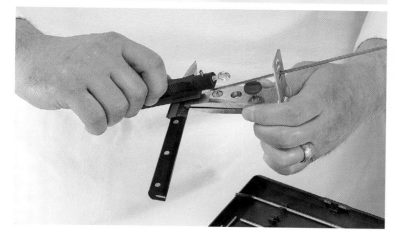

SHARPENING WITH WATERSTONES OR SANDPAPER

Sharpening with waterstones or sandpaper uses an edge-trailing stroke (see page 194).

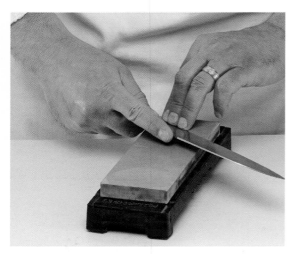

Lay the blade on the stone with the handle at about five o'clock to the stone. Grip the handle with your sharpening hand and place your forefinger on the spine of the knife and your thumb on the back of the blade. That locks your wrist into position.

Press two or three fingers of your free hand lightly on the back side of the knife and lift the spine to your desired angle.

Mentally divide the blade into sections about the width of the fingers you have pressing into the edge and make a smooth forward and back stroke, sharpening only that first section. Use more pressure on the forward stroke and less on the return stroke. Slide the knife and your fingers over to the next section and repeat, working your way from heel to tip. Remember to lift the handle a little to accommodate the curvature of the edge near the tip.

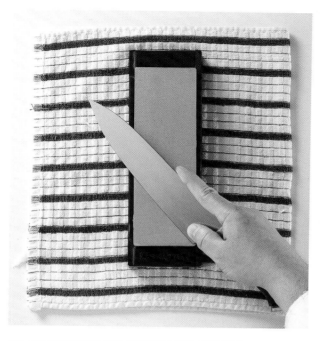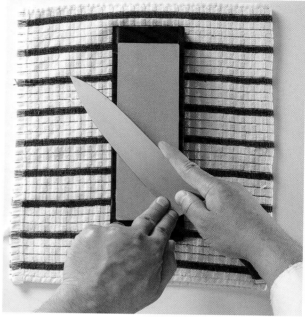

STROPPING

Stropping can be used to finish off a burr (see page 187) and put a final, screaming sharp polish on your edges. The brown strop is a leather hone from HandAmerican.com. The green strop is an inexpensive double-sided strop from Lee Valley Tools charged with green chromium oxide compound.

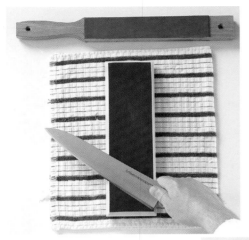

Stropping with a leather hone involves an edge-trailing stroke, sweeping backward from heel to tip using very light pressure.

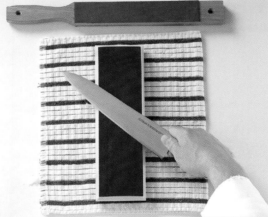

46

As with the waterstone/sandpaper technique (if you opt not to switch hands), the position of the handle changes when working the back side of the knife. The handle begins perpendicular to the hone at the three o'clock and works back to the five o'clock position at the end of the stroke.

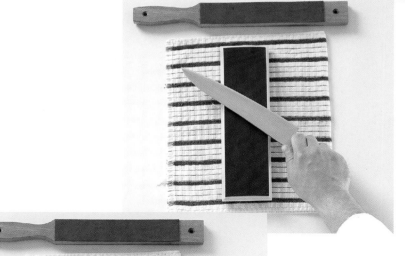

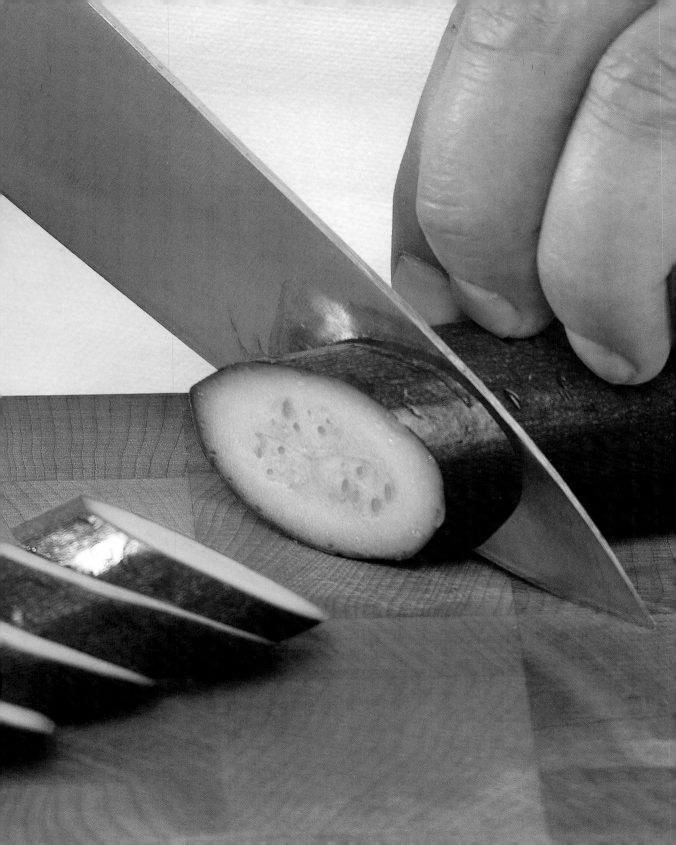

(This is about the only way to cleanly dice bacon; otherwise it just slithers all over the cutting board.) Buy thick-cut bacon that comes stacked rather than fanned out in the flat package. If you have a one-pound package, simply cut a quarter of it off the end. I keep a supply of bacon cut into quarter-pound chunks in the freezer just for cooking. If you have the fanned-out package, stack several slices on top of one another until you have a quarter pound and wrap in plastic.

2. Wash your leeks well. Leeks are a member of the *Allium* family, along with onions, garlic, shallots, and scallions. Like most members of the family, leeks come in layers. Unlike the other members of the family, leeks suck up lots of dirt and sand that gets trapped between the layers. For the more elegant version of this soup use just the white parts of the leeks. Even if you choose to use the pale green parts too, trim off the fibrous dark green tops, rinse, and save them for stock. Cut off the root end and discard. Slice the trimmed leeks in half lengthwise. Fan each piece out like an open book under running water and rinse away any dirt or sand caught in the layers. Slice each leek across the grain into $\frac{1}{8}$-inch slices. When you want a leek or onion to break down in cooking (which we do in this soup) you can facilitate things by cutting across the grain. When you want it to hold together (as for a side dish), cut with the grain.

3. Remember the Flying Hand Trick when making your horizontal cuts on the onion (see Color Plate 18). This is the part that freaks most people out, but if you place your palm on top of the onion and spread your fingers so that they curve out and upward a little bit (like flying your hand out the car window when you were a kid), you'll be perfectly safe.

4. If you want a perfect dice on the potato, square it off first, trimming each side flat and parallel so you have a rectangular block of potato. Cut ½-inch planks from the block. Stack two or three planks at a time and cut ½-inch batons lengthwise, from which you can produce perfect ½-inch cubes when you cut across. Perfection is not a necessity for this soup. The potatoes will break down anyway. But this is practice, remember?

BE URBANE AND DEBONAIR; ROAST A TURKEY

TERMES OF A KERVER (TERMS OF THE CARVER)

breke that dere	break (dice) a deer
spoyle that henne	spoil a hen
fruche that chekyn	fruche (break or crush) a chicken
unbrace that malarde	unbrace a mallard
unlace that conye	unlace a coney (rabbit)
dysmembre that heron	dismember a heron (yes, this one scares me too)
dysfygure that pecocke	disfigure a peacock (ditto)
wynge that partryche	wing a partridge
mince that plover	mince a plover
thye that pygyon	thigh a pigeon
chynne that samon	chine (fillet/remove the backbone) a salmon
splaye that breme	splay a bream
traunche that sturgyon	tranche (slice) a sturgeon
tayme that crabbet	tame a crab

A selection of proper terms for artfully dismantling a variety of meats, fish, and fowl from *The Boke of Kervynge*, the 1508 runaway best seller from Wynken de Worde.★

★Soon to be made into an action movie starring Samuel L. Jackson and one of the Baldwins, I hear.

Not so very long ago, a gentleman was expected to know how to properly carve a roast or whole goose at the table. Not so very long before that, carving was held in such high regard that it was the culmination of a noble education. In the medieval world, young gentlemen of high station were sent to households of (preferably) higher status to be trained in the intricacies of courtly life. They started as table servants and worked their way up through waiter, cup bearer, server, and, finally, carver, picking up the nuances of etiquette and intrigue along the way. The ability to carve was considered more important than learning Latin or philosophy. The carver was expected to use his two knives (the Italians had carving forks, the English didn't) with skill and style to present the dishes, each with its own unique carving technique, in bite-sized portions to the lord and lady.

Carving has always been a source of anxiety, especially to us peons who don't have a noble household education or professional servants (or these days, a degree from a culinary school) to draw upon. As late as 1848, one cheery little book, *The Hand-book of Carving: with hints on the etiquette of the dinner table*, said, "Nothing can be more disagreeable to one of a sensitive disposition than to behold a person at the head of a well-furnished board, hacking the finest joints and giving them the appearance of having been gnawed by the dogs." Self-help books have always preyed on the fear of appearing uncultured or uneducated. That fear is the root of the Thanksgiving or holiday dinner stage fright we have all felt at one time or another when expected to carve the roast beast. Carving a goose, turkey, or rib roast just isn't something we do that often anymore. Now that you know how, get roasting! A basic roast turkey or chicken makes for a simple weekend dinner, and you'll look like a genius as you suavely serve your guests from the carving platter. Once they realize that you can carve like an expert, they'll assume that you can do other things as well, such as repair a vintage Bentley or work the international currency market. ▲

Chicken under a Brick
(Pollo al Mattone)

TECHNIQUES: spatchcocking

SERVES 4

COOKING TIME: about 1½ hours
(including resting)

This Tuscan classic produces crackling crisp golden brown skin and moist, flavorful breast and thigh meat—all in less than an hour. If the weather is nice, you can grill the spatchcocked chicken. Indoors, a heavy cast-iron skillet is ideal. The trick is weighting the flattened chicken so that it makes full contact with the grill or pan. If you do not have a large cast-iron pan, use the biggest, heaviest sauté pan you have. Plan ahead so you can marinate the bird overnight. Choose a smaller 3- to 4-pound broiler/fryer rather than a larger roasting chicken. The meat is more tender and cooks more quickly. One chicken can serve up to four people. Pair with a simple summer salad of diced tomatoes and cucumbers, minced shallots, and chiffonaded basil with a light vinaigrette.

- 1 small (3- to 4-pound) chicken trimmed of excess fat, giblets removed
- ¾ cup (or so) extra virgin olive oil
- 5 to 6 garlic cloves, peeled and crushed
- 3 to 4 tablespoons coarsely chopped mixed fresh herbs (rosemary, thyme, oregano, and basil)
- 2 tablespoons fresh lemon juice

Canola oil (optional)

- 2 bricks wrapped in heavy foil, or another heavy pan or pot filled with water

The night before, spatchcock the chicken, removing the back-bone and keel bone. Flatten the chicken as much as possible so that it will make even contact with the pan or grill. (Whack it with a mallet or the bottom of a heavy pan, if necessary.) If you're cooking in a pan and it is large enough, you can leave the chicken intact. If not, cut through the breast to create two halves.

Place the chicken with the olive oil, garlic, herbs, and lemon juice in a heavy zip-top plastic bag. Squeeze out as much air as possible so the chicken is nearly vacuum sealed in the marinade. Place the bag in a bowl or pan to catch any possible leaks and refrigerate overnight, or at least 4 hours.

If you are grilling, make sure that your grill grates are clean and lightly oiled. When you are ready to cook, make a two-tiered bank of coals★ in your grill or preheat your oven to 450°F. Place your cast-iron pan, if using, over medium-high heat. Heat the pan with a tablespoon or two of canola oil (or any oil with a high smoke point) until shimmering and just beginning to smoke. Remove the chicken from the marinade and let the excess drip free. Remove any garlic or herbs stuck to the skin, or they will burn. Discard the marinade.

Place the chicken, skin side down, in the pan or on the grill and immediately weight it down with the bricks. Close the lid of the grill or turn the heat under the pan down to medium. After about 15 minutes on the grill or 20 to 25 minutes in the pan, the skin should be crisp and deeply golden brown. If not, let it crisp about 5 minutes more. Remove the bricks.

On the grill, carefully turn the chicken skin side up and move it to the indirect heat side. Replace the bricks and close the lid. On the stovetop, carefully turn the chicken skin side up and return the pan to the oven. Roast for another 15 minutes, or until an instant-read thermometer shows 165°F in the thickest part of the breast. Let the chicken rest for at least 20 minutes before serving.

★A hotter, more intense side with a thick layer of coals and a less intense area of fewer coals for indirect cooking.

Salmon Two Ways

TECHNIQUES: Skinning Salmon, Julienne, Concassé

SERVES 4

COOKING TIME: 10 to 20 minutes

This can be a simple grilled or broiled salmon dish with sautéed vegetables brightened up with tomato concassé and capers, or a sophisticated fillet en papillote *(cooked in parchment paper). Salmon is an oil-rich fish that holds up well to grilling or broiling but it also works wonderfully in a more delicate preparation like* en papillote. *All vegetables should be cut to 2- to 3-inch lengths before julienning.*

1	large tomato
2	tablespoons capers
2	tablespoons fruity extra virgin olive oil
1	medium zucchini
2	medium carrots
1	medium leek, white part only
½	bulb fennel
1½	to 2 pounds salmon fillets
	Olive oil
	Salt and pepper
1	tablespoon butter
	Thyme sprigs

Broiler or Grill: Peel, seed, and cut the tomato into small dice, ¼-inch cubes. Mix with the capers and olive oil. Cover and set aside.

Julienne the zucchini, carrots, leek, and fennel. Set aside.

Skin the salmon and portion into 6- to 8-ounce fillets. Brush with olive oil and season with salt and pepper. Heat the broiler or prepare the grill.

Broil or grill the salmon fillets until just cooked through, 3 to 4 minutes per side depending on thickness. Let rest while you cook the vegetables.

Film a sauté pan with olive oil until it shimmers. Add the butter and when it has melted, add the vegetables. Sauté the vegetables for 3 to 5 minutes, or until just tender. Season with salt and pepper.

To serve, lay each fillet on a bed of julienned vegetables and garnish with a tablespoon of the tomato concassé and a sprig of thyme.

En Papillote: Prepare the tomato concassé, julienne the vegetables, and skin and portion the salmon as above.

Preheat the oven to 425°F. Cut four sheets of parchment paper about 15 inches long. Brush the inside of each sheet lightly with oil. Place the julienned vegetables in the middle of one half of the parchment and top with a salmon fillet. Season the fillet with salt and pepper and top with a sprig of thyme.

Fold the other half of the parchment over and make a series of overlapping folds all the way around to crimp the edges tightly and seal the packet. Repeat with the other fillets. Place the packets on a sheet pan and bake for 8 to 10 minutes, or until the parchment is puffed and lightly brown.

To serve, place each packet on a plate and cut an X in the top to let the steam to escape. Allow each person to open his or her own papillote.

Shoestring Fries

TECHNIQUE: Allumette

SERVES 1 (if no one is looking) or 4 if you share
COOKING TIME: 25 to 30 minutes, working in batches

There are several challenges to making decent french fries at home. If you've tried it, your fries probably came out limp and pallid, or brown and greasy. The problem is that really good french fries should be fried twice, once at a lower temperature (about 325°F) to remove moisture from the interior and allow the starch granules to fluff up, and then again at 375°F to brown and crisp the exterior. Then there is the problem of heat recovery. Adding cold potatoes to hot oil drops the temperature precipitously, leading to soggy, nasty fries. Restaurants have quick-recovery fryers filled with a cubic boatload of oil. You probably don't. As you might have suspected, we can get around these problems with a little creative cutting.

Shoestring fries—allumettes (al-yu-MEHTS) or match-sticks to the French—cook quickly enough that the center becomes light and fluffy as the exterior crisps to golden brown. Steam from the moist interior creates a barrier that keeps the oil from penetrating the fry and making it greasy.

4 russet (Idaho) potatoes
About 1 quart peanut, canola, corn, or grapeseed oil
   (they all have relatively high smoke points)
2 tablespoons cornstarch
Popcorn salt or table salt (kosher salt is too coarse to
   stick well)

Refrigerate the unpeeled potatoes for at least 2 hours before cooking. This converts some of the starches to sugars that will brown nicely in the oil.

Peel the potatoes and square them off, or at least cut a flat side to keep them stable on the board. Slice the potatoes into long ⅛-inch planks using your chef's knife or a mandoline or V-slicer.

Cut the planks into uniform ⅛-inch sticks. Normally this would be called julienne but because we're dealing with potatoes it is an allumette. Those wacky French.

If you are cutting the potatoes ahead of time, keep them in a bowl of cold water in the refrigerator. However, they must be very, very dry before frying.

Pat the matchstick potatoes dry with paper towels or spin them in your salad spinner. Toss lightly with the cornstarch and place on a wire rack or clean newsprint to finish drying while you heat the oil.

In a heavy deep★ Dutch oven, deep fryer, or heavy-bottomed pot, heat the oil to 375°F. Use a candy, deep-fry, or instant-read thermometer to keep track of the temperature. Add the potatoes a handful at a time, separating the shoe-strings as they hit the oil. Do not crowd the oil. Watch the

★Make sure that the top of the pot is *at least* 3 inches higher than the top of the oil. Deeper would be even better. If the potato sticks are still a little wet, the oil can foam up and over a shallow pan, possibly igniting on the burner below. Even if you have a pot three feet deep, keep the lid and a fire extinguisher handy. You should have one in the kitchen anyway.

temperature. If it drops to 325°F stop adding fries and let it recover.

Cook until golden brown, 3 to 4 minutes. Remove with a skimmer or tongs and place them in a large bowl lined with a double layer of paper towels or newsprint. Salt liberally. Toss the fries in the bowl to distribute the salt.

Part Three
STAY SHARP

6

THE ART AND SCIENCE OF MAINTAINING YOUR KNIVES

"The best way to ruin your knives is to try and sharpen them yourself."

"Send your knives to a professional sharpener once a year."

"You have to spend hours hunched over a heavy hone slathered with oil."

This well-intentioned advice is parroted in cooking classes, on television programs, in cookbooks and countless magazine articles. And it is just plain wrong. What is especially offensive is when some TV chef spends an hour encouraging you to attempt culinary wonders—like his three-day preparation for authentic French cassoulet (including deboning a rabbit)—then insinuates that you are not quite bright enough to sharpen your own knives. That, of course, should be left to professionals.

Complete and utter *merde*.

Just like cooking, sharpening your own kitchen knives is

not shrouded in mystery. It just takes a little understanding and practice. With some basic background knowledge, a couple of helpful hints, and some inexpensive tools, knife sharpening can be easy and extremely rewarding. Relax. You can do this. You'll have the best edges you have ever encountered and you won't screw up your knives. I promise. It's certainly a lot easier than preparing that cassoulet.

THE SAD TRUTH ABOUT KITCHEN KNIVES

To an ardent cook there is nothing more important than his knife. It is not only an extension of his hands, it is an extension of his very personality. The knife is a chef's paintbrush.

So why are most kitchen knives so bad?

The knives found in most commercial and home kitchens are like supermarket tomatoes—designed more for sturdiness than quality. Knife manufacturers make a series of compromises calculated to keep the largest number of people happy for the longest period of time. That means knives that don't rust, that hold an acceptable edge, and are soft enough to take some serious abuse without breaking. These compromises are not for *your* benefit. They keep the manufacturers from having to deal with too many returns. Because of these compromises, very few people truly love their knives once the shiny factory edge has worn down.

The first compromise begins with the steel. Steel is the heart of the knife. Most manufacturers use variations on a couple of basic stainless steels that are slanted more toward stain and wear resistance rather than holding a razor-sharp high-performance edge. In the kitchen, that's not a bad tradeoff. For the most part you do want a knife that won't rust if you inadvertently leave it soaking overnight. But this compromise is compounded by a heat treatment that leaves the steel much softer than it could be. In general, the harder the steel, the keener the edge it will take. However, a hard steel makes it a little more difficult to get that edge in the first place. So manufacturers leave the steel a little soft, which theoretically makes sharpening at home easier. You just have to do it a lot more often because the soft steel won't hold its edge very well.

Upper-end kitchen knives—like the Wüsthofs, Henckels, and Sabatiers you commonly find in gourmet stores—are a little better, but at 52 to 56 on the Rockwell C scale are still softer than they need to be. By contrast, traditional Japanese knives tend to be between 61 and 64 on the Rockwell scale and are known for their screaming sharp edges. A Rockwell hardness of 56 is the bare minimum you should accept. A rating somewhere between 58 and 62 is perfect—hard enough to take and hold an amazing edge, yet not so hard as to be overly brittle.

The next compromise is in the factory edge angles. Most kitchen knives come with an edge somewhere between 22 degrees and 25 degrees per side, sometimes even greater. If you add the two sides together you get a 50-degree included (total) angle. And that's the best-case scenario. Take a look at a protractor if you happen to have one lying around. Fifty degrees is extremely wide. An angle that chunky is more appropriate for an axe than a chef's knife. The theory is that the hefty angles will allow the edge to resist damage better, which is partly true. It just won't cut worth a damn. The theory is that thick edges—larger angles—are sturdier and will last longer, which is what the majority of the knife-buying public wants. But it doesn't work out that way. Thinner edges actually outlast thicker edges.

But we can't blame everything on the manufacturers. The knives in many home kitchens are subjected to tremendous cruelty and misuse. While I'm certain none of *you,* dear readers, would ever use the sharpener on the back of an electric can opener, cut on a glass or granite cutting board, store your knives

A knife's edge is made of two angles that meet in the middle. When you read that a knife has a 22-degree angle, that's for one side. The "included angle," or total edge angle, is the sum of both sides.

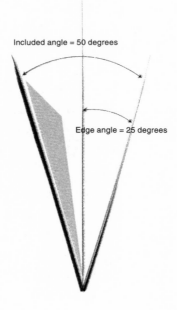

Included angle = 50 degrees

Edge angle = 25 degrees

loose in a drawer, or allow them to be beaten to death in the dishwasher, it does happen. That's why mass-market cutlery is designed the way it is—to withstand this kind of abuse. Unfortunately, when you add soft steel and wide angles to the hard life that knives see in the kitchen, you have tools that are more suited for bludgeoning oxen than fine-dicing a soft tomato.

That's the bad news. The good news is that we can fix these problems. Geometry is far more critical than steel. While you can't change the steel your knife is made from, you can certainly change its geometry and keep your knives at peak performance without too much difficulty. With some basic knowledge and the willingness to invest a little time, you can expect a dramatic increase in knife performance.

EDGE BASICS

Before you start sharpening, you need to determine what kind of blade profile and edge you have. There are two basic blade

STOP THE ABUSE! GENERAL KNIFE CARE

- Use wood, rubber, or plastic cutting boards only. Glass, ceramic, marble, and steel will cause the edge to roll or chip. Don't do it.
- Don't drop your knives in the sink. Not only is it a hazard to the person washing dishes, but you can also blunt the tip or edge. Wash your knives one at a time by hand.
- Don't put your knives in the dishwasher. The heat may damage the handles and the edges will bang against other cutlery or plates.
- Keep your knives clean and dry. Do not put your knives away damp or wet.
- Use a knife block, magnetic strip, slotted hanger, in-drawer tray, or edge guards. Do not store your knives loose in a drawer. The magnetic strip is not recommended if you have small children or inquisitive pets.
- Finally, your knife is not a can opener, a screwdriver, a trowel, a wire cutter, or a hammer. Your knives are for preparing and sharing food. To use them in inappropriate ways is to bring shame to your family. Protesters will gather in your driveway. People will throw refuse on your lawn. Legitimate cutlery retailers will shun you. ▲

profiles, flat ground and hollow ground. Most kitchen knives are flat ground, meaning that the blade tapers directly from the spine to the edge in a wedge shape. At the thin end of the wedge are the bevels that actually form the cutting edge. Hollow ground knives have concave edge bevels beginning halfway down the blade width or lower. Hollow grinds are common on outdoors knives and pocket knives and even on high-end custom knives, but are rare in the kitchen. They do sometimes show up on the low-end kitchen knives you might buy at the grocery store. Granton-edged knives or knives with kullens (the shallow oval grooves intended to keep foods from sticking to the side of the knife) are sometimes incorrectly called hollow ground.

Edges come in a variety of flavors. The most common are the V-edge, the convex edge, the compound beveled edge, and the chisel-ground edge. You are most likely to encounter a V-edge or a compound beveled edge on your kitchen knives. These two edges are variations on a theme. On a V-edge, oddly enough, the edge bevels form a V, two flat surfaces intersecting at a line of (ideally) zero width. A compound bevel takes this idea a little further, using multiple edge angles to maximize cutting performance. A very basic compound edge uses two edge angles, starting with an angle that is more acute than you want the final edge to be. This is called a back bevel or relief angle. You then add a slightly wider angle on top of it, right at the very edge. This is called the primary bevel, though you'll sometimes see it referred to as a microbevel because it is so narrow—$\frac{1}{16}$ to $\frac{1}{32}$ inch down to just a few thousandths of an inch wide. The back bevel's purpose is to thin the metal behind the cutting edge to reduce the thickness of the wedge and increase cutting performance. The thinner the edge, the greater the cutting ability. Adding the small, slightly more obtuse primary bevel gives the edge' strength to avoid damage from impacts, chipping, or rolling. The back bevel also solves one of the great problems with V-edges, the fact that the metal behind the edge gets progressively thicker as the knife is sharpened over time. The knife cuts less well and becomes harder and harder to sharpen. The answer is to grind the shoulders off the edge at an acute angle, that is, add a back bevel, then reestablish the primary bevel.

The convex edge (sometimes called an apple seed or clamshell edge) arcs in a rounded curve down to the edge. The final edge is the intersection of two arcs, creating a very strong edge with more metal behind it than the standard V-edge. Convex edges are generally formed on a slack belt grinder by

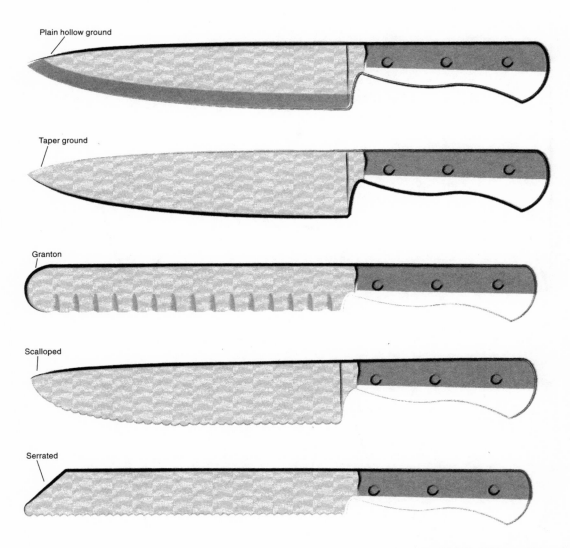

Plain hollow ground

Taper ground

Granton

Scalloped

Serrated

Most kitchen knives are flat ground, though hollow ground edges are sometimes found on low-end kitchen knives.

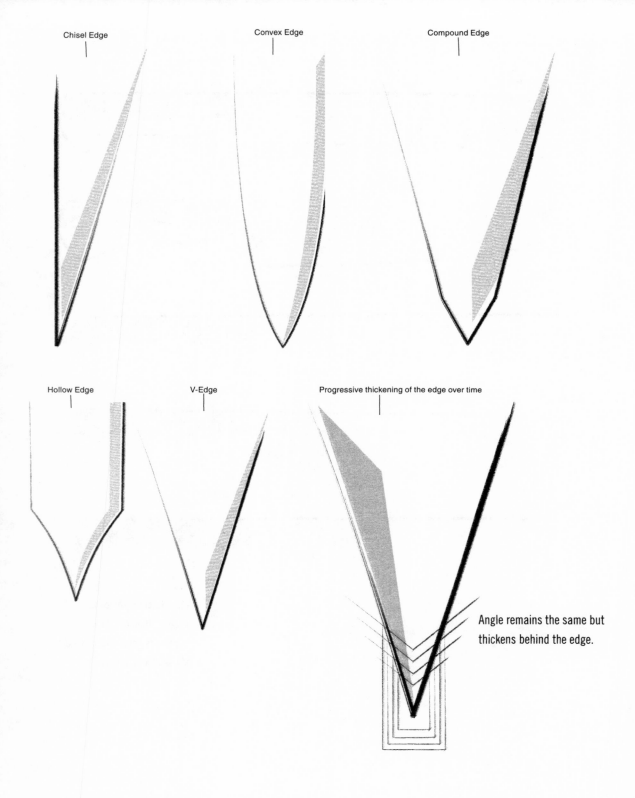

Chisel Edge

Convex Edge

Compound Edge

Hollow Edge

V-Edge

Progressive thickening of the edge over time

Angle remains the same but thickens behind the edge.

the maker, so they can be difficult for the home sharpener to re-create. It can be done, however. You just need to know the Mouse Pad Trick found on page 160. Some sharpening systems use multiple angles to create a compound bevel that mimics a convex edge.

Chisel-ground edges are primarily found on traditional Japanese knives such as the yanagiba (sashimi knife), usuba (vegetable knife), and deba (heavy-duty fish-cleaning knife). The edge is ground only on one side. The other side is essentially flat. Actually, the back side is usually slightly concave so that when you lay the back of the knife flat on a sharpening stone the center of the knife arches above the stone. That allows you to sharpen only the outer edges, saving a lot of time and wear and tear on the knife. It is an ingenious approach. Because chisel-ground knives have a bevel on only one side, they come in right- and left-handed versions. Chisel-ground edges can be extremely thin and sharp. If the edge bevel is ground at 15 degrees and the other side is 0 degrees, you have an included (total) angle of 15 degrees—considerably more acute than the average Western knife.

Single-Chisel Bevel

Traditional Japanese knives are concave on the back.

THE WHOLE TOOTH AND NOTHING
BUT THE TOOTH: MICROSERRATIONS

Books and articles on sharpening often refer to tiny teeth on the edge of the knife. You can actually see them through a microscope. The question is, do you want them there?

Sharpening by its very nature creates a pattern of parallel scratches on the edge of the knife. The coarser the stone, the coarser and deeper the scratch pattern will be and the larger the teeth. Conversely, the finer the stone, the finer and more polished the edge will be with less prominent microserrations. In general, you want the smoothest, most polished edge you can produce with your given sharpening equipment. It is more work on your part but the results are worth it.

While a coarser edge has its uses outdoors (cutting rope, for example), in the kitchen a more polished and refined edge cuts better and lasts longer. The more polished the edge, the more planar and less jagged the surface. If the two sides are rough, they can't come together to form a clean edge.

A clean, well-polished edge will last longer. It's simple physics. Force equals pressure over area. A knife edge a thousandth of an inch thick★ with one pound of pressure behind it concentrates 1,000 pounds of pressure per square inch at the edge. A rough, microserrated edge is like a series of points, a fine row of needles. Each of those points is under tremendous pressure and wears or rolls as you cut. That's a formula for short edge life. However, the more polished the edge, the more you move away from microserrations and toward a continuous edge (or at least a greater number of smaller points).

★An edge a thousandth (.001) of an inch thick is pretty sharp; however, your knives can be even sharper. A thousandth of an inch is equal to 25 microns (25μ). With practice you can get your edges down to about a half micron (.5μ) width, about the sharpness of a razor blade. By comparison, a human hair averages about 50 microns.

Each point is now under less pressure. So a polished edge holds longer because the pressure is distributed over a larger area. It's like lying on a bed of nails. Ten nails will really hurt. A thousand nails works pretty well.★

On the other hand, while it won't last as long, a toothier edge will feel more aggressive. The most extreme example of this came when I was testing a pull-through sharpening device with two spring-loaded coarse rods (like crossed grooved steels). Pulling the knife through left the edge looking almost serrated. You could actually see the grooves scratched into it. Using this device was (I presume) like taking a hit off a crack pipe. The edge became very, very aggressive and felt like it was cutting like crazy, but it died by the end of 20 minutes of prep work. Then I had to go back to the pull-through device for another hit. A polished edge doesn't have the tactile feedback that a coarse edge does. It doesn't *feel* as sharp or like it's doing as much work, but it is.

WHY EDGES WEAR

Your knives are going to get dull at some point. With proper maintenance you can stretch that out for quite a while, but it's still going to happen over time. If you want your edges to last as long as possible, it helps to know how an edge wears and becomes dull. The ability of a knife to hold an edge is affected by several factors, including the properties of the steel it is made from and how the knife is used. The properties of steel that concern us most in the kitchen are strength, wear resistance, and toughness.

Strength is directly related to the hardness of the steel. It is the ability to resist deformation. In a kitchen knife, that means that a hard knife will hold an edge longer because the

★I borrowed this analogy from ABS Master Bladesmith Bob Kramer because it sums up the concept so brilliantly.

edge doesn't roll over as easily as the edge on a softer knife. The downside to increased hardness is brittleness. An extremely hard knife is more prone to chipping. The most extreme example of this is ceramic knives, which are extremely hard and strong but will shatter like glass if dropped on a stone floor.

Wear resistance—the ability to resist abrasion—is affected by the hardness and strength of the steel, but comes primarily from the amount, type, and distribution of carbides in the steel. Wear resistance not only affects how slowly the edge wears down in use, but also how hard the knife is to sharpen. In other words, a knife's sharpenability (is that even a word?) depends more on the type of steel and the type of carbides it contains than on the hardness of the steel. Chromium, vanadium, and tungsten, for example, form very tough, abrasion-resistant carbides. Sharpening, by its very nature, relies on abrasion. You rub Knife A on Rock B. Steel with a lot of tough carbides is going to be more difficult to abrade. That's why a low Rockwell, low-carbon stainless-steel knife from the grocery store can be such a pain in the butt to sharpen while a super hard plain carbon sashimi knife can take a screaming edge in minutes.

Toughness is the ability to resist impacts, chipping, and cracking by bending rather than breaking. While we want our kitchen knives to be hard, we also want them to be tough enough to withstand the occasional whack against a plate or the edge of the sink.

As a general rule, strength and toughness are inversely related. The harder the steel, the less tough and more brittle it is. It will not withstand chopping through bone as well as a tough, slightly softer steel. A tough steel might roll its edge if it encounters significant resistance against the cutting board or is forced through something like a butternut squash—stresses that a strong steel would easily resist.

Didn't know you were in for Metallurgy 101, did you?

Stick with me. We're almost done, and this stuff will come in handy when you settle in to sharpen your knives.

How long your edges last depends mostly on you. In the kitchen, the life of the edge is often determined more by its misuse rather than its use. To put it another way, untrained knife users will put knives in a drawer without using blade guards or an in-drawer rack. They will cut on glass cheese boards. They will leave a knife lying in half an inch of water in the bottom of a roasting pan overnight. They will hit bones, ceramic plates, carving forks, and staples (yes, staples) far more often than we might. So the life of the edge is defined more by its accidental impacts and general abuse than the wear qualities of the steel or a particular sharpening method.

How the knife holds up under use (and even abuse) is a function of wear resistance, strength, and toughness. Toughness is required to resist chipping when you are cutting through materials where you might encounter bone or other hard bits and pieces. Strength is required to resist rolling and denting if, for example, someone in your kitchen (despite repeated warnings) uses a glass cutting board. Wear resistance becomes important for edge holding when you're cutting through abrasive materials like lemongrass or leeks (which can hold a lot of sand).

The most common culprits that put wear resistance, strength, and toughness to the test are:

Wear: Duh. It is a minute factor, but unless you cut only soft foods, your edge will always wear somewhat. However, most wear in the kitchen will come from sharpening your knives. Significant wear will take years.

Indenting and rolling: As pressure is put on the edge of the blade (and remember, the edge's *job* is to concentrate tremendous amounts of pressure), the edge can roll over to one side or the other. This is the most common form of dulling in the kitchen, which is why you need to use your steel or honing rod frequently.

Chipping: The edge can chip or crack under impact, especially when encountering hard materials like bone. Micro-chipping can be an important factor in edge degradation, although most kitchen knives are fairly tough.

Corrosion: Knives take a real beating in the wet, acidic environment of the kitchen. Even if you can't see it, microscopic rusting and the attack of acidic foods can lead to a loss of sharpness in short order. That is why even though non-stainless carbon steel can take a better edge, knives made of stainless steel (at least the high-carbon types) are a better choice in the kitchen.

Technique: Good technique and adequate knife skills will go a long way toward keeping your edges sharp. Glide through the cuts rather than banging the knife into the cutting board. Work around bones and through the gaps in joints when deboning. Your knives will thank you.

7
MAINTENANCE

One of the worst kitchen mistakes you can make is to allow your knives to become dull. When your knives are dull you have to remove metal to make them sharp again. This is time consuming and shortens the life of your knives. Simple routine maintenance prevents both of those things. Doing nothing more than steeling your knife on a regular basis will keep your knives at near-optimal sharpness for a very long time.

> **The blade will only work as well as you are prepared to maintain and sharpen it. It is a symbiotic relationship. You have to take responsibility and actively participate in bringing that knife to its full potential.**
> —**MURRAY CARTER**, 17th Generation Yoshimoto
> Bladesmith

STEELING YOUR KNIFE

That metal rod thingie that came with your knife set is called a steel or honing rod. Unless you purchased your steel separately, you probably ended up with a medium-grooved steel. That's okay, but a finely grooved steel is better. A completely smooth steel or high-grit ceramic honing rod is even better still. Whatever kind of steel you have, using it regularly is the best way to keep your knives ticking along at peak performance. The simple act of swiping your edge down a steel once a week or so will keep your edges sharp for up to a year before they need sharpening again. Whenever you use your knife, especially softer kitchen knives, the edge can roll over a little. It is still sharp, it just isn't pointing straight down anymore. Turn the knife with the edge pointing to the ceiling under strong light. The edge itself should be invisible. If you see glints of light, those are spots where the edge has rolled or folded. Using the steel or honing rod realigns the edge of the knife, forcing the rolled spots back into line and making the edge usable again.

The edge is still sharp; it just isn't pointing straight down anymore.

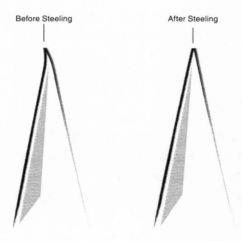

Before Steeling

After Steeling

Be aware that the medium-grooved steels that come with knife sets must be used with a very light touch. A grooved steel acts as a file when used with a heavy hand, knocking microscopic chips out of your edge.

The standard image we all have of steeling a knife involves a chef with his knife in one hand and steel in the other, blade flashing and ringing as the chef clangs it back and forth. If you're particularly adept at this type of swordsmanship, have at it. It impresses the tourists. A more effective method is to stand the steel straight up with the tip resting on a folded towel to keep it from slipping. Why? Geometry.

Place the knife edge against the steel with the blade perpendicular to the steel and you have a 90-degree angle between the edge and the steel, right? Rotate your wrist so that you reduce the angle by half to form a 45-degree angle. Reduce that by half for 22.5 degrees, and you are exactly where you need to be to steel your knife. Most factory edges are somewhere between 20 and 25 degrees per side. You generally want to steel your knife at the same angle or at a very slightly steeper angle than the edge bevel itself.

You can also use the Paper Airplane Trick to make a guide to prop against your steel so you know you are hitting the proper angle. Take a piece of paper and fold one corner over (catty-corner) to the opposite side. Line up the edges and smooth down the crease, very much like making a paper airplane. You've just created a 45-degree angle. Fold the creased side over to the far edge again and you've created a 22.5-degree angle. Sound familiar? Twenty-two and a half degrees is pretty close to 20 degrees, at least as close as you can generally hold a specific angle by hand. This folded piece of paper can serve as a guide for steeling your knife, setting an angle on a sharpening stone, or just checking that you're keeping your angle steady as you sharpen. The paper edge guide is especially handy when you are learning to steel your knives properly. It helps build the correct angle into muscle memory so you can do it without the guide when you have some practice.

When you're steeling, lock your wrist and stroke the knife from heel to tip by unhinging at the shoulder—it's your pivot point. Slowly swipe the knife down the steel by

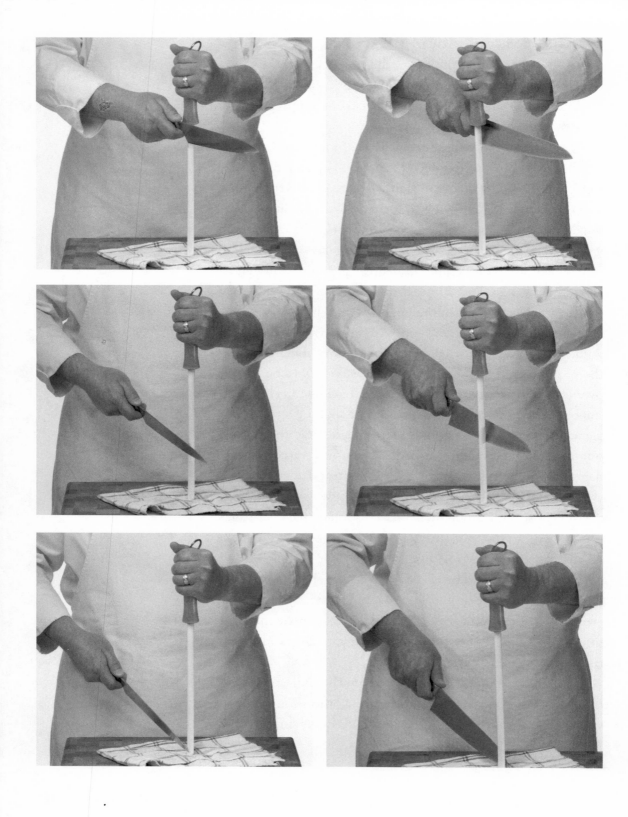

dropping your forearm. The key is to maintain a consistent angle all the way through the stroke. By locking your wrist and elbow, you will keep your angle stable from top to bottom. Follow all the way through the tip but don't let the tip slide off the steel or you'll risk rounding it over time. You don't have to press very hard to realign the edge. Steeling requires barely more pressure than the weight of the knife itself. Alternate from side to side, keeping the same alignment and angle on both sides. It really only takes five or six strokes per side to keep your knife ready for more work. There are pull-through steels for those who aren't sure of their steeling technique. These offer a way to steel your knife at a guided angle. The downside is that the rods are usually more coarsely grooved than is best for your edge, with the Chef's Choice Steelpro being a notable exception. Pull-through steels are limited to fairly wide factory edge angles. Another type of pull-through steel uses weighted rods that glide your edge back into alignment. If the rods are smooth rather than grooved, this type of steel does a nice job keeping your knives in top shape. You still don't have any control over the angle, however. That is set by the manufacturer.

Pull-through steels will give your knife an aggressive edge but it won't last very long. The Chef's Choice Steelpro (left) is finely grooved, but you are still limited to factory angles.

Mousetrap steel from Razor Edge
Systems.

When should you steel? Ideally, you'd give the edge a
stroke or two on the steel every time you take a knife out of
the rack. Truthfully, though, steeling once a week or so is
probably sufficient for the average home kitchen. You should

RELAXATION EFFECT

Another reason to steel your knife before using it rather than after is
the "relaxation effect." This is the mysterious tendency of an edge
to relax into a previous state. So if you steel your edge and put the knife
away, you could pull out the knife next time to discover that the edge
isn't as sharp as you remembered. The freshly honed edge has relaxed
a little and isn't quite so keen. It's better to refresh the edge just before
you use it. The reverse holds true. If you dull your knife in heavy use, let
it sit overnight and you may discover that it is in better shape than you
thought. This will save you some sharpening. There is a lot of anecdotal
evidence for the relaxation effect but not much empirical scientific
study. It's just one of those fascinating things you encounter when you
explore the far reaches of sharpening. ▲

also steel before sharpening your knives so that any rolled or impacted edges are pushed back into alignment. That way you don't cut off the rolled edge and lose more metal than you really need to.

This type of steeling applies to European- and Western-style knives only. The harder steel in Japanese-made knives will chip if steeled on a grooved steel. Traditional Japanese knives should only be sharpened and touched up on water-stones. Japanese-made Western-style knives should only be steeled on a high-grit ceramic rod—which will also work wonders on European-style knives. That is why I prefer them to grooved steels.

TYPES OF STEELS

Knife steels and honing rods come in a variety of sizes, shapes, and flavors. There are round steels, oval steels, grooved steels, smooth steels, diamond steels, and ceramic "steels." If you purchased a set of knives, it probably came with a round, medium-grooved steel. Be careful with this beast. Kitchen knives are reasonably tough and resist chipping fairly well, but a medium-grooved steel can really put that to the test if used with a heavy hand. The grooves in the steel create tiny points of contact with the edge. A smaller contact area makes for greater pressure on the edge. Used lightly, a grooved steel can realign the edge of your knife. Use too much pressure, however, and a grooved steel will act as a file and take micro-scopic chips out of your edge. Your edge will feel sharp because it is now, in effect, serrated, but it won't last very long.

Smooth steels, sometimes called butcher's steels, are several steps above grooved steels. A smooth steel will gently push the metal of the edge back into alignment. It will take longer than with a grooved steel, but you don't run the risk of damaging your edge. A smooth steel is very easy to use and fairly forgiving of sloppy angles.

Smooth steels and high-grit
ceramic honing rods are kinder to
your edges than the grooved steels
that come with most knife sets.

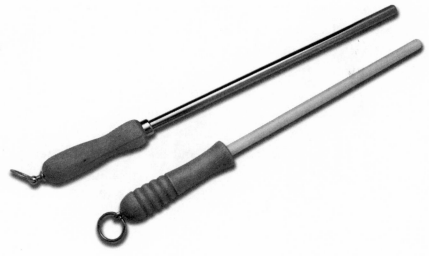

Steel pushes the edge back into alignment without removing any of the weakened metal that might be at the very
edge. A ceramic honing rod will remove some of the weakened steel while also aligning the edge. The edge will be
more stable and stay sharp for much longer. There is micro-
scopically more metal removed with the ceramic and diamond rods, but it is so little that you won't notice any
difference even in years of constant use.

8

SHARPENING FUNDAMENTALS

Before we get into the actual mechanics of sharpening, it helps to understand some of the basic principles:

- the burr
- sharpening angle
- abrasive
- consistency

These principles apply no matter what sharpening method you choose.

THE BURR

Embrace the burr. The burr is your friend. A burr, sometimes called a wire edge, is a rough, almost microscopic, raised lip or ridge of metal that forms when one side of the edge meets the other while you are sharpening. It is the only way to be absolutely certain that you have fully ground that side all the way down to the edge. In short, you grind Side A until it meets Side B and pushes up a small curl of metal. If you stop sharpening before the burr is formed, the two sides might not meet cleanly and your knife will not be as sharp as it could be. This is the problem with sharpening instructions that advise a certain number of strokes per side. Without raising a

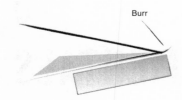

The burr always forms on the side opposite the edge you are sharpening.

burr, there is no way to know if the number of strokes has been effective in removing metal all the way to the edge. Learning to raise and detect a burr is the most important step in keeping your knives razor sharp.

Sometimes you can't see the burr, but you can always feel it. You check for a burr on the side opposite the edge you have been grinding. So if you are sharpening Side A, you will push a tiny lip of steel over so that it sticks up on Side B. To find the burr, hold the knife blade horizontally and stroke your fingertips or the pad of your thumb perpendicular to the edge, pulling gently down and away. Stroke *across* the edge, not along it. The burr can be very sharp, and you don't want to lop off a finger. You can also check for a burr by pulling the edge backwards across your thumbnail. The newly sharpened side will feel smooth. The burr will scrape and catch. Remember, check the side *opposite* the one you've been sharpening. You are checking for a very light lip caused by the edge folding over to the other side. Check at various points along the edge. The burr tends to form quickly at the base of the blade but takes a little longer at the tip. You must feel a burr running all the way from heel to tip to know that you have fully ground that side of the edge.

THE ANGLES

The 50-degree total angle that comes standard on many kitchen knives is way too obtuse. You can do much, much better than that, even on inexpensive kitchen knives. However, the better the steel, the thinner and more acute you can take the edge without risk of damage. For the vast majority of kitchen knives, 15 to 20 degrees per side will provide a significant increase in performance without requiring any additional maintenance. Dedicated slicing knives can be taken down to 10 to 15 degrees per side. You can go even lower and improve the performance of any knife but the edge may require more frequent touch-ups.

A good compromise in the kitchen is a 15/20 compound bevel. That is a 15-degree back bevel with a 20-degree primary edge face. This is a sturdy edge that will outperform any factory edge but is still suitable for kitchens where the knives may be used carelessly. If your knives are not subject to mistreatment at the hands of your children or inept brother-in-law, a 10/15 compound bevel is even better.

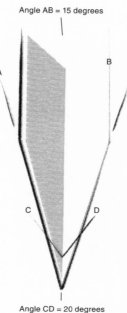

Angle AB = 15 degrees

Angle CD = 20 degrees

I FIND YOU ABRASIVE

You sharpen your knives by scraping away metal. That's really all there is to it. But there is a tremendous variety of abrasives available.

Traditionalists still demand an Arkansas stone. These stones were originally mined from a novaculite (from the Latin *novacula*, meaning "razor stone") deposit in Arkansas, though novaculite formations also exist in Oklahoma and Texas. These stones are graded from softest to hardest as Washita, Soft Arkansas, Hard Arkansas, and Black Hard Arkansas. Many Arkansas stones are now made with ground novaculite reconstituted into benchstones; however, natural mined Arkansas stones are still available.

Synthetic aluminum oxide and silicon carbide stones are very hard and don't wear like natural stones. They clean up easily with a scouring pad and are more consistent in their grading systems. Norton, Spyderco, and Lansky manufacture synthetic stones in a variety of grits and sizes. Norton calls its silicon carbide Crystolon. Their aluminum oxide stones are called India stones.

Japanese waterstones are considered by sharpening experts to be the ultimate sharpening tools. Woodworkers have been using them for years to put extreme edges on their tools, and now waterstones are migrating into the kitchen. Although natural waterstones are rare and hard to find, reconstituted and synthetic stones are readily available. These reconstituted waterstones are held together by resin, clay, or ceramic bonds. They cut very quickly (and wear quickly as well) and are available in extremely fine grits that will put a high polish on an edge. Waterstones must be soaked before using and they do need to be flattened occasionally, which makes them more of a bother than other sharpening systems. The waterstones made by Shapton are considered top of the line but they can be very expensive. King, Naniwa/Ebi, Bester, Penguin, Ice Bear, Suehiro, and Masahiro brands are all good, as are the Norton waterstones that can be found in any home improvement store in America.

Synthetic waterstones like those used in the Edge Pro system are formulated from aluminum oxide, but like Japanese waterstones they are designed to be used wet to cut most effectively.

Diamond "stones" have man-made diamond particles imbedded in or coated on a base metal. They cut very aggressively and should be used with a light hand. Diamond hones were formerly available only in very coarse grits, but that is changing rapidly. EZE-Lap, Lansky, and DMT make excellent diamond hones. There are two types of industrial diamonds used in these stones, monocrystalline and polycrystalline. Polycrystalline diamonds are less expensive, but they wear quickly. Monocrystalline diamonds wear much more slowly and are a better purchase over time.

All of these stones come in a variety of shapes and sizes. Some are cut to fit a particular sharpening system. Others are intended to be used alone on a countertop or workbench. These are referred to generically as benchstones, whatever abrasive they are made from.

Sandpaper is an often-overlooked sharpening medium. The fine grits needed for good knife sharpening aren't usually found at the local home improvement store, but they are stocked at woodworking shops and automotive supply stores and are readily available online from vendors like HandAmerican.com, which offers a complete sharpening system based on sandpaper and leather strops. The good stuff—silicon carbide wet/dry sandpaper—is inexpensive and can be had in grits ranging from an extremely coarse 100 grit to the very fine 2500 grit. You can even find Mylar-backed microfinishing film down to 0.3 microns,★ which will put a mirror polish on the edge of a knife. Sandpaper comes either plain or backed with pressure sensitive adhesive (PSA). PSA sandpaper is easy to stick to a thick plate of glass (hey, finally a real use for that glass cutting board!) or granite tile. It can be reused several times before it needs to be replaced. Wet/dry sandpaper is the basis for the Mouse Pad Trick.

There are two other issues related to abrasives that must be considered: grit and lubrication.

You Want Grits with That?

All of these abrasives come in a variety of grits from very coarse to ultrafine. Grit refers to the size of the individual particles of abrasive in the sharpening stone. A stone with a finer grit has smaller particles and produces a more polished edge with less prominent microserrations. A stone with a coarser grit has larger particles, produces an edge with more prominent microserrations, and tends to abrade metal away more quickly. There are several different grit rating systems, and unfortunately they a little difficult to correlate. For example, Japanese waterstones are graded differently than diamond stones and both have different numbering systems than the codes found on powered grinding wheels or sandpaper.

What you need to get started is a coarse-to-medium stone for shaping the edge and removing the shoulders of overly thick edges. You'll also need a fine stone for sharpening and polishing the final edge. The double-sided combination stones found

★That's 0.00003937 inches to you and me. Yow.

THE MOUSE PAD TRICK

Do you have an old mouse pad? Is there an auto supply store nearby? You can make a superb sharpening system for about $5. Go to your nearest auto supply store and get a sheet or two of silicon carbide wet/dry (sometimes called waterproof) sandpaper. You might even be able to find it in the automotive section of a large department store. This is the stuff used to sand automotive paint between coats. Buy the self-stick kind (PSA-backed) if they have it. You need at least 600 grit, but if they have higher grits get those, too. The next step up is usually 1200 grit. Go nuts. It's cheap.

Stick the sandpaper to the mouse pad and trim the edges. This is your new sharpening system. This system requires using an edge-trailing stroke. That means that unlike other sharpening methods, you don't push the edge into the sandpaper, you pull it, leading with the spine of the knife. Imagine an old barbershop with the barber stropping his razor, stroking away from the edge. That's the idea. To determine your angle, lay the knife flat on the pad, edge toward you. Lift the spine slightly while pulling very lightly toward you. Continue lifting until the edge just barely bites into the sandpaper. That's your angle.

Keep the edge at that angle and stroke the knife away from you, spine first, moving from heel to tip. When you reach the end STOP and lift the knife straight up off the sandpaper. Don't roll it off or lift the spine further or you'll mess up the edge you're creating.

Turn the knife over and stroke back the other way with the edge away from you, pulling the spine toward you at the same angle as the previous stroke. The really cool thing is that the mouse pad is soft enough that it conforms to the angle of the knife edge. As long as you're pretty close you'll be fine. This will give you an amazing edge in a fairly short amount of time. If you want to polish it up, remove the coarse paper and stick down the higher grit sandpaper and do the same thing. Do not press down much more than the weight of the knife or the mouse pad will roll up over the edge and round it off.

Because the mouse pad is soft, it deforms lightly around the edge of the knife and gives you a slightly convex bevel. A convex edge has many advantages but can be difficult to achieve without a belt sander. This is one way to create or maintain a convex edge without serious power tools. Sticking the sandpaper to a flat surface like a glass plate or large granite or ceramic tile from the home improvement store will create a V-edge. You will need to put the sandpaper and whatever you decide to stick it to on a raised surface to give you sufficient clearance for your hand. Find a dictionary or a piece of two-by-four or just place the mouse pad at the edge of the countertop so the knife's handle can hang off. You need the handle of the knife far enough above the work surface so your fingers don't drag and change the sharpening angle. ▲

in most hardware stores, the kind with a rough side and fine side, just won't do the trick. The coarse side isn't coarse enough and the fine side isn't fine enough. Any of the sharpening systems mentioned later will come with appropriate stones.

In very general and imprecise terms, stones rated lower than 300 grit are coarse, 300 to 400 are medium, 600 up to 1200 are fine, and 1200 and up are extrafine.

Japanese waterstones have their own grit rating system. They cut so quickly that anything below 800 grit can be considered coarse, although they'll leave a much more polished edge than a corresponding Western stone. You can consider 1000 to 2000 grit medium and medium-fine; they make excellent general-purpose stones. Waterstones can go up to 30,000 grit, but that's overkill for kitchen purposes. Finishing with a 4000 to 6000 waterstone will put an astonishing edge

COMPARING ABRASIVES ACROSS A SAMPLING OF SHARPENING SYSTEMS

JAPANESE WATERSTONES	SANDPAPER (U.S./ISO)	EDGE PRO*	SPYDERCO SHARPMAKER 204	LANSKY	DMT DIAMOND	ARKANSAS STONES	PARTICLE SIZE IN MICRONS (APPROXIMATE)
	80/P80			XC70			200
120	120/P120	120C		C120	XXC120		120
	180/P180						82
	220/P220		Diamond				68
220					XC220		60
				M280			50
320	P320				C325		45
	320/P400						35
500						Washita	29
600	400/P600			F600	F600		25
700		220MF				Soft	21
800	500/P800		Medium (gray)			Hard	20
1000	600/P1200			UF1000		White Hard	15
	800/P1500						12
1200	1000/P2000	320EF	Fine (white)		EF1200	Black Hard	9
1500	P2500					Translucent	8
2000			Ultrafine				7
3000	5 micron microfinishing film	800UF					4–5
4000		2000 polish tape					3
6000							2.5
8000–12,000	1 micron microfinishing film	6000 polish tape					1–2
15,000							.95
30,000	Chromium oxide polishing compound						.5

*Edge Pro synthetic waterstones are marked in U.S. grit but are listed on the chart according to their cutting speed and level of polish compared to Japanese waterstones, which they most closely resemble.

on your knife. By the way, not all waterstones are Japanese. American-made Norton waterstones are an exceptional value.

The stones that come with Spyderco's Sharpmaker are listed as medium (the gray stones) and fine (the white stones). The gray stone is the equivalent of an approximately 800 grit waterstone, the white to a 1200 grit waterstone in the level of polish they create on the edge.

The synthetic waterstones from Edge Pro systems are also somewhat idiosyncratic. The coarse stone is labeled 120, the medium-fine 220, extrafine 320, ultrafine is 800. However the grit rating does not correspond to their cutting speed or the level of finish they leave on the knife. They are more closely related to Japanese waterstones than to the more pedestrian synthetic stones. Conversations with the owner of Edge Pro reveal that the 320 extrafine stone is equivalent to a 1200 grit Japanese waterstone and the ultrafine equivalent to a 2500 grit Japanese stone. The basic system comes with a medium and a fine stone, which should be sufficient for most needs, though the coarse stone comes in handy for quickly reshaping bevels and the finer stones leave a near-mirror finish.

Like Oil and Water

While it is traditional to lubricate the top of a sharpening stone with oil, most modern stones and sharpening systems work best dry. The purpose of a sharpening stone is to grind the edge and remove metal. Oil reduces friction and makes the process much slower. In theory, oil helps float away metal particles that would otherwise clog the pores of the stone. In reality, you are dragging your edge through a slurry of metal and stone particles with each stroke, potentially causing microscopic chipping. If you have already used oil on your Arkansas stone, you'll probably need to keep using oil. But if you have a new Arkansas stone, a diamond stone, or a synthetic stone, go ahead and use it dry or with just a little water.

It will be less messy and work much better. Synthetic stones clean up with a scouring pad and abrasive cleanser.

Waterstones are another matter entirely. Both natural and synthetic waterstones require water in order to cut effectively. Japanese waterstones can be damaged if used dry and must be soaked thoroughly before use. Waterstones wear very quickly, revealing new layers of cutting abrasive as the swarf is washed away. That's why waterstones are so effective. There is always a new layer of sharp abrasive cutting away at the metal of your edge. (By the way, *swarf* is one of those cool terms you get to toss around when you discuss sharpening. Swarf is the slurry of metal filings and stone grit that builds up as you sharpen. Throw that into your next cocktail party conversation and just watch the expressions of awe appear as people realize that you are a sharpening *genius*.)

CONSISTENCY

You must be able to maintain a consistent angle while you are sharpening. This can be a little tricky, which is why there are so many gimmicks and sharpening systems on the market. These systems don't provide any magic. All they do is help you keep your edge at the same angle throughout the sharpening session. It takes experience and practice to keep the edge at a constant angle stroke after stroke using only your hands and eyes. It can be frustrating, but it is very much like learning to type—you've got to slow down and concentrate on precision. Speed comes with repetition. The more consistent you can hold the angle, the closer you come to the ideal of two flat planes meeting at a point of zero width.

Learning to sharpen freehand on bench stones is the Zen mastery level of sharpening. It is extremely rewarding, but if all you want is a good edge on your kitchen knives there are dozens of ways to cheat your way to success. We will cover all of them.

9

YOUR FIRST EDGE
(I'M SO PROUD)

In the next chapter we will cover high-performance edges. A high-performance edge is reasonably easy to achieve, but does take a little more time and effort. The result, however, will be unlike anything you have ever experienced in the kitchen. But if you are not quite up for kitchen revelations at the moment or if you just need to touch up your chef's knife before your dinner guests arrive, this quick start will get you going. We are not going to cut in a new edge, just sharpen the existing one. You can get your knife shaving sharp in about 15 minutes. All you have to do is remember the basics—abrasive, angle, consistency, and burr.

GET READY

Abrasive

First, what are you going to sharpen with? What are your abrasives? If you don't need your knife sharpened immediately, check out the sharpening systems (chapter 12) to find which method or system is right for you. If you are in a hurry and already have a stone or two in the house, use those.

Remember, you need something medium or medium-coarse to grind in the edge, and you need a fine abrasive to smooth out the scratch pattern and create a finely honed edge. If you have nothing with which to sharpen but need a sharp edge quickly and with little investment, you can use the Mouse Pad Trick on page 160.

Angle

Now we have to figure out the sharpening angle. At this point we are just trying to match the existing edge angles, not create new ones. The best way to do that is the Magic Marker Trick (page 168).

In a pinch, you can assume that your knife was originally ground somewhere between 20 to 25 degrees per side. Every sharpening system in existence has a setting in that range. Try the closest setting and use the Magic Marker Trick to adjust up or down.

If you are sharpening freehand, you can still set the correct angle quickly and easily. With a standard chef's knife or santoku, lay the knife flat on the sharpening stone and lift the spine about ⅔ inch (measured opposite the heel) and you'll be at the right sharpening angle. You can use a ruler or you can simply use a stack of eight quarters★ as a reference. For a paring knife, raise the spine about ¼ inch (a stack of 4 quarters). Either way, simply raise the spine of the knife until it is resting on the stack. Use the Magic Marker Trick and add or subtract coins as needed until you are wiping the marker off the width of the bevel without being too low or high. That is your sharpening angle.

★Nickels are about the same thickness as quarters, so you can use a combination of the two if you don't have the right number of quarters in your change jar. For those of you with calipers, 8 quarters is not quite ⅔ inch. It's more like .55, while ⅔ is .66. The difference is made up by the thickness of the spine of the knife.

COIN TRICKS

A U.S. quarter coin is officially .069 inches thick, though they vary a little. Nickels (.077 inches) are so close to the thickness of quarters that you'd have a hard time telling the difference without calipers. In practical terms, that means you can set an edge angle using stacks of nickels and quarters and be within thousandths of an inch of where you need to be. Four quarters is a little more than .25 inch, 5 quarters is about .33 inch, 6 quarters is about .4 inch, 7 quarters is just under 1/2 inch, and 8 quarters is just over 1/2 inch (and matches the factory angle on many chef's knives if you rest the spine on the stack). Ten quarters is slightly over .66 or 2/3 inch high. It takes a surprising 15 quarters to reach a full inch high.

A stack of quarters serves as a good reference for setting your edge angles.

Just place the stack of quarters on your sharpening stone and raise the spine of the knife so that it rests on the stack just opposite the heel. If you want to be really fussy you can take the width of the spine into account, too. On a chef's knife, that means subtracting a quarter. So to raise the spine of a chef's knife almost exactly 1/2 inch, use 7 quarters rather than 8. The thickness of the spine from the outside to the centerline is about the same thickness as the eighth quarter.

Traditional Japanese sharpening techniques call for two coins for the back bevel and three coins for the primary edge. Compare that to the 8 to 10 quarters required to match the factory edge on most Western chef's knives and you can see what good steel and a commitment to regular maintenance can net you. ▲

THE MAGIC MARKER TRICK

One of the easiest ways to ensure that you are matching an existing bevel is to coat the edge with a felt-tip marker. Even on a dull knife you can see where the edge was ground by the factory. Tilt the knife back and forth under a light. The edge bevel will appear as a narrow, bright line. Paint only the edge. Try not to stray above it. Wait for the marker to dry a little and make a stroke or two down your stone (or slide the stone down your edge, if you are using one of the rod-guided systems). As the marker is wiped away by the sharpening stone you will be able to see where the stone meets the edge and whether you have matched the angle properly. If the marker is wiped off over the width of the bevel, or if the wiped area is at least centered in the marked section, you have matched the angle properly. If your angle is too wide, the spine is too high and only the marker near the very edge will be removed, leaving a strip of marker behind it. If your angle is too shallow, the spine is too low and only the marker near the shoulder, above the edge, will be removed. Recoating the edge as you sharpen is a good way to ensure that you're holding the correct angle throughout the process. No matter what type of sharpening system you use, the Magic Marker Trick will save you a lot of time and frustration. ▲

Consistency

Maintaining consistency depends on your sharpening system. Any sort of guided system sets the angle for you and holds it constant. V-systems and crock sticks simply require you to stroke straight up and down. If you are sharpening freehand on a bench stone or sandpaper, you can use a ruler or stack of coins as a guide. Keep the quarters nearby and place the stack on your sharpening stone every stroke or two to make sure you are holding a consistent angle.

Burr

When you have figured out how to ensure a consistent angle, you are ready to sharpen. This is where you will meet your new best friend, the burr. Remember, a burr is a very fine raised lip of metal that curls up *opposite* the side you are sharpening. You can feel it by pulling your fingertips or the pad of your thumb very lightly across and off the edge. You can also pull the edge backward across your thumbnail. Areas where the burr has formed will catch and feel rough on your fingertips or thumbnail. The burr tells you when you have fully ground the bevel all the way to the edge.

HERE WE GO: STEP-BY-STEP BASIC SHARPENING

Set up your sharpening system or sharpening stones following the manufacturer's instructions. Use a felt-tip marker and the Magic Marker Trick to determine your sharpening angle.

If you are using a Spyderco Sharpmaker, place the medium rods in the 20-degree slot. If you are using a rod-guided system like a Lansky or Gatco, put the rod for the medium stone in the 20- or 25-degree setting (whichever gives you the right results with the marker trick). If you are using a clamp-on edge guide, attach it to the knife so the spine is raised about half an inch (or whatever setting matched the bevel using the Magic Marker Trick). If you are using benchstones freehand (without some sort of guide), you can use a ruler, stacks of coins, or the Paper Airplane Trick (discussed on page 149 in the section on steeling your knives) as a visual reference to determine how high to raise the spine above the stone.

Each type of sharpening system has its own way of moving the edge over the stone or vice versa. You stroke the edge straight down with V-systems or crock sticks. Rod-guided systems glide the stone over the edge at a predetermined angle. The technique that requires the most practice is sharpening on benchstones, so I will describe the process in detail.

To make best use of a benchstone, place it on a rubber-footed base or damp towel so it doesn't slide around (just like a cutting board). There are two ways to place the stone, lengthwise with one of the narrow ends facing you and the length of the stone extending away from you, or horizontally with the stone parallel to the edge of the countertop or workbench. Either way, stroking from the heel of the knife to the tip makes it easier to see the angle you are setting. Working from corner to corner on the stone allows you to use the full length of the stone most effectively. Grip the knife with your forefinger along the spine and thumb on the blade on the pull or right-to-left stroke. Place your thumb on the spine and forefinger on the blade on the push or left-to-right stroke. This will lock your wrist into position and help keep your sharpening angle consistent.

Place the heel of the knife on the stone. Raise the spine to your desired angle and glide the full length of the knife across the full length of the stone, sweeping from heel to tip. You'll need to raise the handle slightly at the last third of the stroke to follow the curve of the edge up to the tip. Resting the fingertips of your free hand lightly on the blade will help you stay steady as you arc the knife across the stone. You do not need to use very much pressure at all. The stone will do the work. Pressing too hard will make it difficult to hold your angle constant. Check your marker stripe to make sure you are hitting the edge bevel cleanly.

Lift the knife off the stone and flip it over, making sure not to drag the edge on the stone. Raise the spine to the proper angle, lock your wrist, and make a smooth sweep from heel to tip in the opposite direction. That's your first pass.

To maintain the aesthetics of the knife, you'll want the bevels relatively even on each side. If you just grind one side

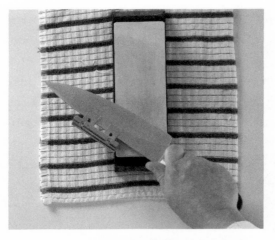
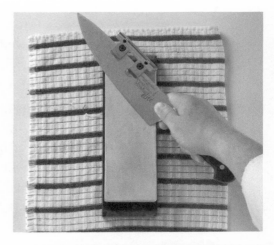
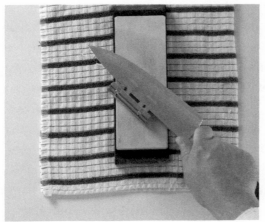
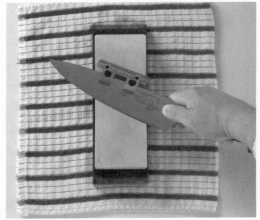

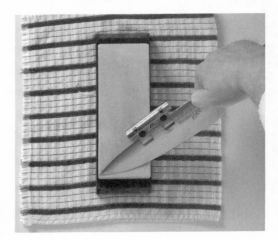

Place your stone on a damp towel so it doesn't slip. The basic stroke is from heel to tip with the edge moving into the stone. The knife moves across the stone from one corner to the opposite corner. Here the knife is clamped into an edge guide to hold the edge at a consistent angle. If sharpening freehand, place the fingertips of your other hand on the spine and flat of the knife to help keep the angle consistent. Lift the handle slightly at the end of the stroke to follow the curve of the edge up to the tip.

until you get a burr, the other side will require much less grinding but the bevels will be mismatched. To keep them matched, sharpen one side for five or six strokes, then switch to the other side, maintaining your angle. Check the edge every time you switch sides to see if you can feel a burr. Keep sharpening and switching sides until you detect a burr beginning to form. Remember, the burr forms on the side opposite from the side you are sharpening. As soon as you detect a burr, stop switching sides. Keep sharpening on the current side until the burr runs the entire length of the opposite edge. Repeat on the opposite side until you push the burr over to the first side along the full length of the edge.

You're almost home. Now that you've got your burr, you need to remove it so that the true edge remains. Technique matters. Stroke gently, alternating sides with each stroke. Lighten up on the pressure as you go. You are trying to thin and center the burr. There is no hard-and-fast rule, but five to ten strokes per side should do it. If your checking reveals that the burr is simply flopping from side to side, lessen the pressure even more. Burrs are funny things. Some knives form a weak burr that grinds right off. Others form a burr that hangs on tenaciously and bends back and forth as you switch sides.

There are sharpening gurus who suggest that you sharpen right up to forming a burr but stop short of actually forming one. That would, in fact, be ideal. Unfortunately, very few people are that good. It is more effective to sharpen to a burr on each side with each successive stone to ensure that the two sides are actually meeting cleanly. The burrs, however, become finer and harder to detect at each level.

There are several methods for removing a stubborn burr. The most effective technique is to do a couple of finishing strokes at a higher angle to cut off the burr, then swipe the edge through a wood cutting board to clean up any remaining weak metal. I use the corner of my butcher block for this. Simply place the heel of the knife on the edge of the cutting board and using nothing more than the weight of the knife, pull the edge through to the tip. The first swipe will leave a dark mark in the wood from the weakened metal coming off the edge. The second or third pass will leave a clean cut, a good visual indicator that you have gotten rid of the burr.

Another approach is to use a very light touch and switch sides of the knife on each pass of the stone. This effectively centers the burr and allows it to be ground away by the next stone. This method works better when you are using a number of finer and finer stones. It is especially effective with waterstones or Edge Pro and Lansky-style systems where you progress through multiple stone grits to a very fine polish.

You can also swish the edge back and forth over a stack of dampened newspaper. This is a good way to get rid of a fine burr but is less effective at coarser grits. Try this with a knife you think is already sharp and you'll be surprised at how much grabbier and aggressive your edge feels.

Now you are ready for the next step. Change from the medium stone to the fine stone. Your job now is to remove the scratch pattern left by the coarse stone and refine the edge. Check your angle to ensure that it is the same for each stroke. The edge from the fine stone should start to appear smoother and more polished fairly quickly. Once the scratches are polished out (about five minutes or so), sharpen on one side until you form a very light burr the full length of the opposite side. Make sure that it extends from heel to tip. Switch sides and form a light burr on the first side. Once you have formed a burr on each side, alternate strokes and reduce the pressure as you proceed. You are trying to polish the burr off. If you press too hard you'll simply form another one.

Finish with one or two extremely light strokes on the fine stone. To make sure that the burr is completely gone, swipe the edge through your cutting board once or twice to remove any weakened metal just as you did with the coarse stone. Then place the knife on the stone and take one last stroke on each side, increasing the angle by just a little—about the thickness of the spine. Make this stroke as light as possible. You should now have an edge that will readily shave the hair on your arms with little tugging. If you hold a piece of paper by the upper corner at about the ten o'clock position, the knife should slice through it easily, leaving a smooth (rather than ragged) cut. If your knife doesn't seem this sharp, you may still have a residual burr. Swipe the edge through the cutting board again and make one or two light passes on the fine stone at a slightly higher angle. That should do it.

Congratulations. In less time than it took to read this section you have created an edge that is far better than when the knife was new. Sharp edges are addictive. You will have to suppress the urge to sharpen everything in the house. Your spatula does not need to be honed to a razor edge. You might not want to share your enthusiasm, though. If your friends and neighbors find out how good you are, they will hound you to sharpen *their* knives.

10

HIGH-OCTANE EDGES

Now that you have a handle on basic sharpening, you are ready to make a massive leap in the performance of your knives. It doesn't take much, just a couple of minor changes in geometry. This doesn't require anything radical. Your knives won't breathe fire or julienne carrots on their own (at least not while you are looking), but for such a minimal effort the rewards are tremendous. It is like making a small adjustment to your stodgy four-door sedan and getting race car performance *and* increasing your mileage to 75 miles per gallon.

THIN IS IN

Most kitchen knives could stand to be thinned out a little. They come from the factory not only with edge angles that are too obtuse, but also with edges that are too thick. There is just too much metal there for them to cut as effectively as they should. That's why compound bevels are a good idea. The acute back bevel thins the steel behind the edge and improves cutting performance.

The blade of a knife tapers—gets thinner—from spine to edge, creating a wedge shape. By thinning the metal behind the edge, you are narrowing the wedge. Manufacturers keep their edges thick and wide for a good reason. Knives get abused badly in many home kitchens. But if you don't plan on abusing your knives by using them as can openers or pry bars, why suffer the bad edges created for those who do?

To be perfectly honest, thinner edges *are* slightly more delicate. That's okay. The performance trade-off is well worth it, and the risks are minimal. Kitchen knives are not survival knives or sporting knives. They don't cut rope or chop saplings. Most cutting in the kitchen involves relatively soft materials. Butternut squash is about as hard as it gets. The life of an edge is affected more by accidental impacts—the occasional bone or edge of a plate—than wear from use.

What is really interesting is that a thinner edge will *outlast* a thicker one and stay sharp longer. The thinner edge starts out performing better than the thicker edge, so even as it wears it has a lot of ground to lose before it falls to the performance level of the thick edge. Thinner edges cut more easily, putting less stress on the edge. Lateral (sideways) and torsional (twisting) stresses are very hard on your edges. The more smoothly and easily you are able to cut, the less stress you put on the edge.

Thin is good.

HOW LOW CAN YOU GO?

Ideally your knife blade should taper down to about .02 inch/.5 mm measured a quarter of an inch behind the cutting edge. Unfortunately, many chef's knives are nearly double that.

The goal is to thin the edge as much as possible, but not so much that it is regularly damaged during hard use. If you are searching for maximum performance, you can thin the edge a little more with each sharpening until it reaches an unacceptable level of fussiness, that is, more steeling than you feel like putting up with. This is easier than it sounds. Once you have established thin, acute geometry, putting a slightly wider final edge on it is just a matter of a couple of swipes down a sharpening stone.

One factor that plays into how thin you can take a knife's edge is the quality of the steel. That's one of the primary advantages to the new breed of hard super steels. You can sharpen them to very acute angles without risk of significant damage. As we've discovered, the average kitchen knife is made from pretty mediocre steel. But it can still be much thinner than the factory edge.

Please note, however, that this applies mainly to the chunkier German and French-style knives. Modern machined knives like Shun, Mac, Global, and many of the Japanese-made Western-style knives are already reasonably thin and are sharpened to about 16 degrees per side. But even they can be hot-rodded to greater performance.

THE COMPOUND SOLUTION

One way to thin the edge is to lay the knife nearly flat on a coarse stone and scrub away metal until you get to the edge. This is easy and extremely effective but it does leave your knives looking like they have been dragged behind a dump truck. A more civilized method is to use a compound bevel. Remember those? A compound bevel is two or more bevels that start with an acute angle and get progressively wider toward the edge. For German and French-style knives you can achieve a quick and easy performance increase with a 15/20 compound bevel—a 15-degree back bevel (or relief angle) and a 20-degree edge bevel. Because the 15-degree back bevel thins the steel behind the edge, the 15/20 edge cuts significantly better than a factory edge. The 20 edge bevel is extremely sturdy and can withstand quite a bit of abuse. Because it is still fairly close to factory angles, a 15/20 bevel doesn't take long to create and you don't have to remove a lot of metal. As an added bonus, nearly every sharpening system

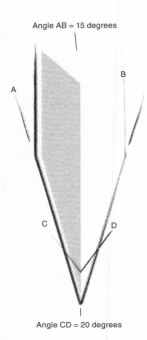

Angle AB = 15 degrees

A

B

C

D

Angle CD = 20 degrees

made has slots or settings to create a 15/20 edge. That's the good news. The bad news is that the 15-degree back bevel will not extend back far enough to achieve ideal geometry. It will, however, knock the shoulders off the overly thick factory edge. You also end up with a 40-degree total angle at the edge, which is still much wider than it could be.

For modern machined knives like Global, Mac, or Shun, which are already at 15 to 16 degrees per side, a 10/15 compound bevel works wonders. That's 10 degrees per side as a back bevel and 15 degrees per side as the cutting edge—total edge angle of 30 degrees, which is still sturdy enough for very hard kitchen use.

With good steel, you can go down to absolutely crazy bevel angles if you don't mind a little extra maintenance. An 8/12 (or even 5/10) compound bevel is perfectly reasonable with VG10 or any other contemporary kitchen steel hardened to at least 58 on the Rockwell C scale. You just have to touch up the edge more frequently and be a little more careful about contact with bones or hard surfaces. An edge this fine shouldn't be steeled. It should be lightly touched up on your finest stone or a leather strop when you notice its performance decreasing. If you go down this far and find that the edge is too fussy for your taste, simply add another microbevel at the very edge. With just a few swipes down a fine stone you can turn your 8/12 bevel into an 8/12/15 bevel, which maintains the high-performance geometry but gives you a more robust edge.

SHARPENING A COMPOUND BEVEL

Sharpening a compound edge is exactly like the basic sharpening you did in the previous section with two exceptions. It takes a little longer and you need a wider array of abrasives. It can be done with just a medium and a fine stone, but taking the relief angle back to 15 (or 10) degrees involves removing more metal than we did before. A coarse stone makes hogging

MAGIC ANGLE FINDER!

Want a 20-degree angle? Divide your blade width at the heel by 3. Want 15 degrees? Divide by 4. That gives you the height above the stone to raise the spine of the knife. Measure the height of the spine above the heel.

DESIRED ANGLE	DIVIDE BY
20 degrees	3
15 degrees	4
12 degrees	5
10 degrees	6
8 degrees	7
5 degrees	11

So if you want to put a 15-degree edge bevel on your 2-inch-wide chef's knife, raise the spine half an inch above the stone: 2 (width of the knife) ÷ 4 (Magic Angle Finder) = 0.5. What if you are metrically inclined and want to sharpen your 45 mm-wide Japanese gyuto to 12 degrees? Check the chart and you'll see that the magic number for 12 degrees is 5. So you would raise the spine of your knife 9 mm: 45 mm ÷ 5 = 9mm.

If you are interested, here's how it works.

Brother, Can't You Read the Sine?

A knife blade on a stone makes a right triangle. The spine of the knife and the stone create a 90-degree angle—two sides of the triangle. The third leg of the triangle is the width of the blade. It is the hypotenuse,

(Continued)

the long side of the triangle. The ratio of the hypotenuse to the opposite side is the sine of the angle. Yeah, it makes my head hurt, too.

So the angle at which the blade edge meets the stone is determined by the width of the blade and the height of the spine above the stone. The sine is the relationship between the two. The sine for a 10-degree angle is technically 0.1736 and change—approximately a 1:6 ratio. The sine for a 15-degree angle is 0.2588—approximately a 1:4 ratio. The sine for a 20-degree angle is 0.342—just about a 1:3 ratio. You see where this is going.

If you divide the blade width by the second number in the ratio you get the height of the spine over the stone, which tells you how high to raise the back of the knife to get the desired angle. ▲

off metal a breeze. Every sharpening system comes with basic stones. Coarser and finer stones are usually an upgrade. They are worth it. Get them.

The easiest way to start is with a 15/20 bevel for the standard German/French-pattern knives and 10/15 for the Japanese-made knives. The difference in the way your knives cut will be immediately noticeable and the process won't eat up your whole Saturday afternoon. Be prepared to spend 30 to 45 minutes including cleanup. Trying to go from a standard factory 25-degree edge to a 10/15 performance edge in one sitting might take an hour or more. It is much easier to go in stages. If you like the 15/20 edge, try taking it down a little more on your next sharpening session and work your way down to a 10/15.

I will use the 15/20 edge as the example. If you are putting a 10/15 edge on your knife, simply use 10 degrees for the back bevel rather than 15, and use 15 degrees as the cutting edge rather than 20.

Remember the basics: abrasives, angle, consistency, burr.

Start with your coarsest stone and establish your 15-degree back bevel angle. If you're using a Spyderco Sharpmaker, put the stones in the 15-degree slots. With a Lansky, Gatco, or Edge Pro system, slide the rod to the 15 degree setting. If you are sharpening freehand or using edge guides, use the Magic Angle Finder to raise the spine to the right height above the stone.

Sharpen exactly as you did in the basic sharpening section. Glide the edge over the stone (or the stone over the edge) in a sweeping arc, heel to tip if you are using a bench-stone. Work in sections as the manufacturer recommends with an Edge Pro or Lansky-type system. Flip the knife over, being sure not to drag the edge on the stone, and sharpen the other side. Alternate sides until you feel the beginnings of a burr. Once you detect a burr starting to form on one side, sharpen the opposite side exclusively until the burr extends the full length of the edge. The burr tends to form at the heel of the knife first. The tip takes longer. There is no need to spend time on the sections of the edge that have already formed a burr. Concentrate on the areas that still need work. Once the burr extends from heel to tip, turn the knife over

---

ADVANCED MAGIC MARKER TRICK

The Magic Marker Trick also comes in handy when you are establishing a back bevel. If you coat the edge before working at the 15-degree setting you can grind the back bevel until the marker is ground *almost* to the edge, leaving a very thin ($1/32$ to $1/64$ inch or .5 mm) strip of marker. That's about how wide the primary edge face will be. Rather than grinding all the way to the edge until you get a burr, you can now switch to the 20-degree setting, knowing that the last little bit of edge will become the primary edge face. You still have to raise a burr at 20 degrees, but the marker trick can save you some time. ▲

and repeat the process on the second side. With a coarse stone all of this will happen fairly quickly. If you use the Advanced Magic Marker Trick you can save a little time on this step.

Take several light, alternating strokes to center and thin the burr. Swipe the edge once or twice through a corner of your cutting board to remove any weakened metal. If you want to dress up the scratch pattern, switch to your medium stone and give the edge several passes on each side (at the same angle) to polish them out a little. Do the same with the fine stone. This is not strictly necessary. You can cut in your back bevel with a coarse stone and go directly to the edge bevel but you will see a very slight performance increase if you take each bevel through whatever succession of grits you are using. The bevels will look nicer, too.

Time to move on to the actual edge bevel. Establish your 20-degree angle. If you're using a Sharpmaker, switch to the 20-degree slots. With a Lansky, Gatco, or Edge Pro system, simply change the rod to the 20-degree setting. If you are using edge guides, unclamp the guide and slide it forward about $\frac{1}{8}$ inch until the spine reaches the correct height. Freehanding, raise the spine about $\frac{1}{8}$ inch. If you switched to your fine stone to clean up the back bevel, switch back to your coarse stone or the next one up, usually a medium stone.

Create a burr again at the new sharpening angle. This time you're grinding the edges to meet at a 20-degree angle. This will happen very quickly because you've already removed most of the metal you need to. The 20-degree primary edge face will be very narrow compared to the 15-degree back bevel, somewhere between $\frac{1}{32}$ to $\frac{1}{64}$ inch or about 0.5 mm. Switch sides and repeat until you have a burr running the full length of the first side.

Time to center and thin the burr again. It should be much lighter this time. Stroke gently from heel to tip, alternating sides with each stroke. Remember to lighten up on the pressure as you go. If your checking reveals that the burr is simply flopping from side to side, lessen the pressure even more. Swipe the edge through the cutting board to remove the last of the burr and take a couple of more strokes on the medium stone.

Change from the coarse or medium stone to the fine stone and continue. Keep stroking side to side until all the scratches from the previous stone are gone. You still need to ensure that the scratch pattern from the fine stone reaches all the way to the edge to give you the sharpest edge possible. The only way to do that is to raise a burr, but you don't want anything but the lightest, finest burr. It should be nearly imperceptible. At this point you shouldn't have to concentrate on one side. A burr should pop up spontaneously after just a few strokes on each side. Continue lightening up on the pressure as you proceed. Swipe the edge very lightly through the cutting board and finish with one or two very light strokes on the fine stone at a slightly higher angle. On a Sharpmaker, tilt the knife in very, very slightly toward the center to increase the angle. Guide the knife down the stone using no more pressure than the weight of the knife itself. A light touch at the end of the sharpening process is the key.

If you have an extrafine or ultrafine stone, now is the time to use it. The thinner the edge, the more it benefits from being refined. Use a light touch. The edge is less than a thousandth of an inch in thickness and the stones are very hard. It doesn't take much pressure to roll the edge over. You don't have to go all the way to a burr, but at this point the edge bevels are meeting so cleanly and evenly that you'll probably get one in just a couple of strokes. You know what to do: center and thin it with very light strokes, swipe the edge very lightly through the corner of your cutting board, and take a couple of light strokes at a slightly higher angle.

That's it! You are done. Resist the urge to oversharpen. Your edge should be frighteningly sharp at this point. It should shave easily and slice newspaper cleanly. Cutting carrots will be a revelation. Cucumbers will quiver in fear and tomatoes will cower at your approach.

This edge is not only very sharp, but is very strong. With regular steeling it will last for many months under hard use, up to a year in household use. When steeling ceases to have the desired effect, it's time to sharpen again. However, now that you've ground the back bevel you really only need to sharpen the primary edge—20 degrees on a 15/20 bevel or 15 degrees on a 10/15 bevel. If your knife is very dull go back to your medium stone. If it is only a little dull you probably get away with starting on your fine stone. The burr will be very easy to raise in subsequent sharpening sessions.

HOW TO TELL IF YOUR KNIFE IS SHARP

How do you know when you have achieved the ultimate high performance edge? Depends on what you want to do with it. Remember sharpness is not only two edge faces intersecting at a line of minimum width, but also is a function of blade shape, geometry, and the material to be cut. We want a keen edge that can hold up in repeated usage while cutting easily and smoothly in the kitchen.

At the most basic level, you can tell when you've set your knife's edge bevels correctly by placing the knife at a 30- to 45-degree angle on your thumbnail and pulling across the edge. A properly set edge will bite in and not slip off your nail. Of course, you could hurt yourself doing this, or at the very least wreck your nail polish. Any slick, slightly rounded surface will do. A plastic pen is perfect. Tilt it at a 30- to 45-degree angle on a countertop and lay the knife edge straight up and down on the plastic, perpendicular to the countertop. Pull the edge from heel to tip. If it bites in, you've set your edge correctly. If it slides off, you have some more work to do. The sharper the blade, the straighter you can stand the pen before the edge slips.

Another test is to take a cotton swab and push the fuzzy head over the length of the edge. The swab will reveal any rough spots in the edge. Any nicks or burrs will pull the cotton fibers loose from the head. A dull edge will feel slick while a sharp edge will bite into the swab.

If you are feeling adventurous, try the Hair Test. Lay the knife nearly flat against the hair on the back of your head and pull gently down. Very gently. An aggressive, keen edge will readily grab the hair. A dull edge will simply slide off. *Don't shave the back of your head.* Just pull gently down to see if the edge catches and tugs. I don't want any irate calls from your barber, hairstylist, or spouse.

The classic test of sharpening is shaving the hair of your arms. This has several problems, not the least of which is that the hair might not grow back or could come in coarser and darker than the surrounding hair. If you have a lot of knives to test you'll end up looking like you have mange. Slicing newsprint is also a good test. Newsprint is thinner and more delicate than copier paper or notebook paper. A knife has to be fairly sharp to cleanly slice newsprint held lightly between the fingers. Hold the sheet by the corner at about the ten o'clock position so the knife slices the paper at a slight angle when swiped straight down. The newsprint should shear cleanly and quietly. Even more challenging is phone book paper or a credit card receipt. They are so flimsy that the knife must be very sharp to slice them without the paper crumpling.

The best test, though, is actually using the knife for its intended purpose. Try a soft tomato or ripe plum. A keen edge will bite into the tomato with little pressure and just a light draw across the skin. This is one area where a slightly toothy edge has an advantage. It will bite faster. A more polished edge may skate a little at first but will cut thinner, cleaner slices. If you have polished your santoku to a mirror-like edge, try dicing a few carrots or potatoes. The reduced effort will be immediately noticeable. If you work in a commercial kitchen or are preparing lunch for a church event you will be less fatigued and your wrist and forearms won't ache after a morning of prep work. Dicing a case of beets will be . . . well, dicing a case of beets is never fun, but it will be less of a chore than it was before.

11

ADVANCED SHARPENING TECHNIQUES

STROPPING

Imagine an old-fashioned barber honing his straight razor on a wide leather belt. That is stropping—using an edge trailing stroke on a piece of leather or canvas. It can do wonders for your kitchen knives. Stropping is a handy way to finish off a burr or put a final polish on your edge. Unlike straight razors, which can be stropped on a hanging belt, knives should be stropped on something with a hard back to prevent rounding the edge. While you can improvise a strop from just about anything from the back of a legal pad to an old belt, hard-backed leather strops are readily available from woodworking shops and online from places like Lee Valley Tools and HandAmerican.com. The strop is usually charged with an abrasive, meaning that you rub a honing compound like green chromium oxide paste into the leather. These compounds contain micro fine abrasives that further hone and refine your edge. Chromium oxide, for example, has abrasive particles about .5 micron in size, making it roughly the equivalent of a 30,000 grit Japanese waterstone.

Like the Mouse Pad Trick, stropping is an edge-trailing

stroke. Lay your knife flat on the strop with the spine facing away from you. Slowly pull the knife toward you while lifting the spine. You don't strop by pushing the edge into the leather because you will cut into the strop. This is just to find the right angle. When the edge just barely begins to bite into the leather you have found your stropping angle. It should be pretty close to the same angle that you used to finish your edge on the stones. Keep that angle as you stroke the spine away from you, pulling the edge along behind. Do not press down. Use only the weight of the knife or the leather will deform enough to curl up over the edge and round it. Even though the edge is moving backward, you still sweep heel to tip across the full length of the edge, and you still lift the handle slightly to follow the edge around the curve to the tip. When you get to the end of the stroke, STOP. Lift the blade straight up off the strop. Do not lift the spine any higher or roll the knife over while it is still on the strop. You can round the edge that way.

Now lay the knife flat again, spine toward you, and gently push the edge toward the end of the strop while lifting the spine. Again, this is just to find the correct angle. You don't want nicks and gouges in your strop, so be gentle. When the edge begins to bite you've found your angle for the return stroke. The return stroke is the same motion as the first stroke, simply in reverse. The edge is facing away from you and you pull the spine toward you, sweeping the knife lightly from heel to tip.

Stropping will create an extremely sharp, highly polished edge. To some extent, stropping can make up for less than perfect sharpening technique because leather is a more forgiving medium.

HANDLING SERRATED KNIVES

Serrated knives and bread knives are a special case. Serrated knives are rarely truly sharp but they will maintain a modest

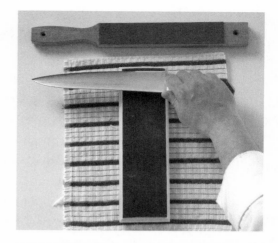
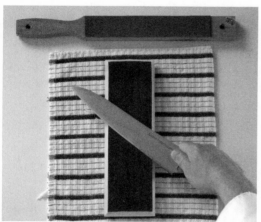
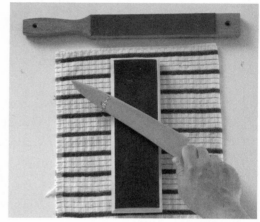

Stropping with a leather hone involves an edge-trailing stroke, sweeping backward from heel to tip using very light pressure. As with the waterstone/sandpaper technique (if you opt not to switch hands), the position of the handle changes when working the back side of the knife. The handle begins perpendicular to the hone at the three o'clock and works back to the five o'clock position at the end of the stroke.

level of sharpness for a very long time because the insides of the serrations don't contact hard surfaces. That's what the teeth are for. The teeth don't just cut, they are also sacrificial lambs offered up to steakhouse swordsmen and children everywhere who feel that if they're not grinding into the ceramic of the plate, they are not cutting their food.

Serrated edges are ground only on one side. The back is usually flat. If your serrated knife feels dull, you can often improve the edge by simply laying the back of the knife nearly flat on a fine stone and removing any residual burr left by the manufacturer. If your serrated knife is truly dull there are four ways to sharpen it. You can pretend the serrations don't exist and sharpen on a stone, sharpening system, or electric sharpener as you would a plain-edged knife. This will eventually remove the serrations. You can sharpen the flat, nonserrated back of the blade at a very low angle. This will sharpen the knife, but also will eventually remove the serrations, though not as quickly as the first method. You can sharpen the serrations individually with a tapered diamond rod, a V-shaped ceramic file, or a small dowel rod wrapped with wet/dry sandpaper. Finally, you can sharpen on a V-system or crock stick setup, going very slowly so the ceramic rod glides in and out of the serrations. This last method works quite well, especially with the Spyderco Sharpmaker. Its triangular rods fit into serrations much more easily than the standard round crock sticks. If you want to keep your serrated knives as sharp as they can be, the Sharpmaker system is the way to go. The Lansky rod-guided system also has a triangular accessory hone for sharpening serrated edges. If you have a Lansky system, this upgrade is definitely worth it.

TRADITIONAL JAPANESE CHISEL-GROUND EDGES

Sharpening chisel-ground or single-bevel knives is not difficult. Traditional Japanese knives like a yanagiba (sashimi knife) have a single wide bevel on the front (right) side of the blade. The back is lightly concave in the center. When you lay the back flat, the center of the blade is arched over the sharpening stone. The back touches the stone along two "ride lines" along the outer perimeter that converge toward the tip. This keeps you from having to sharpen the whole back of the knife. What is especially nice is that these knives give you a built-in angle finder. You simply match the front bevel angle and sharpen as usual—but only on the beveled side. When you raise a burr, you remove it by laying the back side of the knife flat against your stone and cutting the burr off with a stroke or two. That's it. Fairly simple. Mostly. As with all simple things, there are nuances.

Single-Chisel Bevel

Traditional Japanese knives are lightly concave on the back so only the outer edges touch the sharpening stone.

When sharpening Japanese knives, there are no shortcuts.

—**NORMAN KORNBLUTH**, Broadway Panhandler

There are a couple of things to keep in mind that make the process faster and easier. They fall into our basic categories of abrasive, angle, consistency, and burr. Traditional Japanese knives respond best to waterstones. You need at least a

1000 grit stone to set the edge and a 4000 to 6000 grit stone to finish and polish it. A 2000 or 3000 grit stone in between the medium stone and fine stone will make polishing out the scratch pattern go much faster. You can refine the edge up to 16,000 or even 30,000 grit but that is usually reserved for sharpening junkies; 8000 grit is about the practical limit in the kitchen. Waterstones must be used wet. Some require soaking for about 15 minutes before use. A plastic spray bottle is handy for hosing down the stone to remove swarf and rewet the top.

> **A cook should be aware of his or her own habits and style because knives always adjust as they are used by a particular person. They adapt to that person.**
>
> —MASAHARU MORIMOTO, Iron Chef and owner of Morimoto restaurant

While the back of a chisel-ground edge is sharpened flat to the stone, essentially a zero-degree angle, it is still half of the total edge angle and needs to be as polished as the front bevel. The knife can only be as sharp as the polish on the back. One shortcut you can take is to polish the back of the knife first, taking it up through each successive grit starting with the 1000 grit waterstone. Don't worry if a light burr forms on the front bevel. Keep in mind that you don't want to scrub off too much steel. You don't want to widen the ride lines. Finish the back with the highest grit waterstone you have and keep the stone nearby (and wet). Now when you sharpen the front bevel, rather than cutting off the burr on the back with each successive stone you simply use the finest stone. Half the sharpening job is done. The rest goes very quickly.

The other angle-related consideration to keep in mind is that you don't have to sharpen the entire front bevel. While sushi chefs and sharpening masters do exactly that (and would probably burn me as a heretic), you don't have to. Not every time, anyway. You can cheat a little. These knives are sharpened with an edge trailing stroke, like stropping. You lay the front bevel of the knife on the stone with the handle at about five o'clock and press two or three fingers of your free hand onto the back side of the knife right at the edge. That rocks the knife forward, up onto the bevel. Grip the handle with your sharpening hand and place your forefinger on the spine of the knife and your thumb on the back of the blade. That locks your wrist into position. Now cheat. Tilt the knife ever so slightly into the edge, raising the spine just a hair. That allows you to sharpen just the edge of the knife. Instead of trying to sharpen a 15 mm-wide bevel, you are now sharpening a 3-to-5 mm section right at the very edge. You will need to sharpen the whole bevel every third or fourth sharpening session just to keep the geometry correct, but using this shortcut will save a lot of time and effort.

Rather than try to sharpen heel to tip in one stroke, divide the blade into sections about the same width as the fingers pressing on the back. Make one forward stroke down the length of the stone, sharpening just the first section. Both hands should move as a single unit, moving forward together and keeping the knife steady. Bring the knife back the same way, sharpening the same section. Use lighter pressure on the return stroke than the forward stroke. Slide the knife (and your fingers) over to the next section and repeat. As with Western knives, you will need to lift the handle slightly when you sharpen the section near the tip. Once you reach the tip, work your way back along the length of the knife, still working in sections, until you reach the heel. Check for a burr on the back side. When you have one, bring the fine stone out and lay the back of the knife flat on the stone. Place the fingers of your free hand near the edge and your thumb near the spine. Press down evenly and glide the edge into the stone, again working in sections until you reach the tip. You are not trying to form a burr on the front side, just to cut this one off. Repeat this whole process on the next higher stone. Remember, any burr you form must be removed by the finest stone to maintain the polish level of the back.

These knives should not be steeled. They are too thin and too hard. The edge will chip if dragged down the side of a grooved steel. The easiest way to keep the edge in peak condition is to touch it up on your finest stone. This is exactly like sharpening the knife but you don't need to form a burr. Three or four passes down the front side and one on the back should be sufficient to restore the edge to full sharpness.

WATERSTONE/SANDPAPER TECHNIQUE

The sharpening technique used for traditional Japanese single-beveled knives also works for Western-style knives, especially when sharpening on waterstones or sandpaper. Some waterstones are so soft that sharpening with the edge cutting into the stone can gouge the stone. It is just as easy to cut into sandpaper with a careless stroke if the sandpaper is not perfectly smooth on the glass plate or whatever hard backing you are using. The solution is to use an edge-trailing stroke. Just as with the traditional single-beveled knives, you lay the blade on the stone with the handle at about five o'clock to the stone. Grip the handle with your sharpening hand and place your forefinger on the spine of the knife and your thumb on the back of the blade. That locks your wrist into position. Press two or three fingers of your free hand lightly on the back side of the knife and lift the spine to your desired angle. Unlike single-beveled knives, you do not have a preset angle to work with, so you need to use one of the previous techniques to determine how high to lift the spine to hit the correct angle. Mentally divide the blade into sections about the width of the fingers you have pressing into the edge and make a smooth forward and back stroke, sharpening only that first section. Use more pressure on the forward stroke and less on the return stroke. Slide the knife and your fingers over to the next section and repeat, working your way from heel to tip. Remember to lift the handle a little to accommodate the curvature of the edge near the tip.

When you have worked your way back to the heel and are ready to sharpen the other side, you have a decision to make. Switch hands or work backward? The easiest way to keep your angles steady is to change hands and repeat the process in mirror image. If you are right-handed, that means gripping the handle with your left hand and using the fingers of your right hand to guide the edge. This is not as awkward as you might think. The other option is to turn the knife over and change your grip so that your thumb is along the spine and your forefinger is on the flat of the blade. You don't have to switch hands but you do need to change the position of the knife on the stone. Start at the far end of the stone with the handle at three o'clock to the stone. Press two or three fingers of your free hand right at the edge (which is now on the far side of the knife) and raise the spine to the correct height. Pull the knife toward you with moderate pressure on the edge and sharpen the section closest to the heel. Use less pressure on the forward return stroke. Slide the knife over to the next section and repeat. As you work each section, alter the angle of the handle to the stone so that you end up back at five o'clock when sharpening the tip.

When using this technique you still need to follow the basics—abrasive, angle, consistency, and burr. This just gives you a different approach to applying them.

ROUNDING THE SPINE

Something that very few chefs (and even fewer knife makers) take into consideration is the sharpness of the spine of their

Switching hands is not as awkward as it might seem. It becomes very natural with just a little practice.

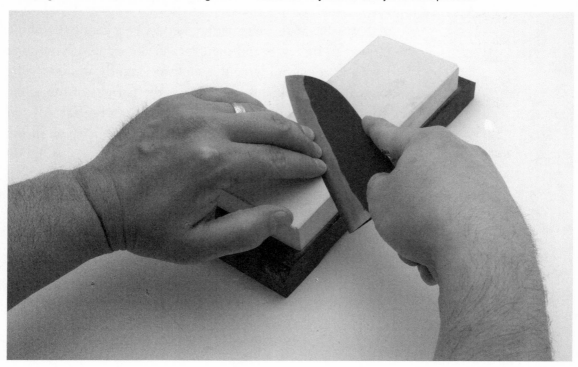

knives, but they should. Ask any chef to show you his knife hand calluses. He will have a thick callus at the base of his forefinger from the Pinch grip used in most kitchens. He may also have another callus on top of the second finger where it rubs against the heel of the blade. He will also have aching hands and possible repetitive stress injuries.

In the interest of economy, most knife manufacturers leave the spines of their knives square. The edges of the spine can be sharper than the knife itself. That edge cutting into your finger will lead to blisters, calluses, reduced circulation, numbness, and injury with extended use.

It doesn't have to be this way. In about 10 minutes you can ease the edges of the spine so that they don't cause blisters, cut off circulation, make your hands numb, or create any of the other discomforts of standard kitchen knives.

Lock your knife, edge down, into a padded vise. The padding doesn't have to be anything elaborate. Two pieces of flat rubber or leather will keep the jaws from scratching the blade. You'll need a sheet of 600 grit (or so) wet/dry sandpaper available at any auto supply store. Use a gentle shoeshine motion to lightly round the edges of the spine. If you don't have a vise you can wrap the sandpaper tightly around a rubber sanding block and scrub across the corners of the spine. You don't have to buff hard or remove a lot of metal. All you need to do is break the 90-degree angle of the spine in the small area where your forefinger rests. You can also lightly round the back of the heel. These simple modifications will make a world of difference in the comfort of your knives.

12

OVERVIEW OF SHARPENING SYSTEMS

J ust like cooking, sharpening is simply a matter of under-standing a little and practicing a lot. And sometimes it in-volves buying more stuff, but that's half the fun, isn't it?

BENCHSTONES AND WATERSTONES

If you'd like to try freehand sharpening or even sharpening with edge guides, get the biggest stones you can afford. A good rule of thumb is to use a stone that is about as long as the long-est knife you intend to sharpen. This becomes a little tricky if you have large kitchen knives. Very few manufacturers make stones that will easily accommodate a 300 mm/12-inch knife. The minimum size to avoid major frustration is 6 by 2 inches. Even better is 8 by 3 inches. Every manufacturer makes stones in about this size.

As with knives, purchase what you need and expand your collection as you gain knowledge and experience. It is not necessary to buy a whole quarry full of stones to get started. At a minimum, you'll need at least one coarse-to-medium stone and one fine stone. If you are on a budget, the best solution may be a combination stone—a coarse-to-medium grit on one side and a fine grit on the other. If you are just getting started, waterstones (Japanese or not) offer the best bang for the buck. They cut quickly and leave a fine polish on your edges. King makes a 1000/6000 combination stone that is nearly ideal for those who want to start sharpening with waterstones. Norton makes a 1000/4000 combination stone that is reasonably priced. Because a 1000 grit stone wears more quickly than finer stones, a better option would be a stand-alone 1000 grit stone and a combination 4000/8000 stone. Other brands to look for include Naniwa/Ebi, Bester, Penguin, Ice Bear, Suehiro, and Masahiro. Shapton stones are regarded by many as the holy grail of waterstones. They range from the extremely coarse 120 grit to the superfine (nearly insane) 30,000 grit. Keep in mind that waterstones wear more quickly than silicon carbide or aluminum oxide stones. Over time they will dish out, becoming concave in the middle from repeated use. Any vendor who sells waterstones will also sell a stone flattener to address this problem. It is a good idea to flatten your stones regularly to prevent any dishing. This applies to all benchstones, not just waterstones.

Many culinary resources suggest a tri-hone, a three-stone sharpening system bathed in oil. If you have one, great! Use the basic strategies (abrasive, angle, consistency, burr) to change the way you go about using the tri-hone and make it more effective. Please note, however, that while the coarse stones are sufficiently coarse to set an edge, the fine stone of most tri-hones is about 280 U.S. grit, or the equivalent of a 320 grit waterstone. This is still very coarse and leaves a ragged edge on your knives. You will need to finish the edges with something at least 600 U.S. grit or a 1000 grit waterstone. Finer would be better.

If oil and water seem too messy, you might consider

diamond benchstones or sandpaper. Diamond stones are available in a multitude of grit sizes from extra coarse (120) to extra fine (1200). They cut very aggressively even at finer grits. Diamond benchstones have the added advantage that they remain perfectly flat. In fact, coarse diamond stones make excellent stone flatteners for your other stones.

Silicon carbide wet/dry sandpaper is inexpensive and versatile. PSA-backed sandpaper can be applied to just about any flat surface to create a sharpening system. Float glass or plate glass is commonly used as a base by woodworkers because it is so flat, but you can also use granite or ceramic tiles from the home improvement store. HandAmerican makes a complete sharpening system using a heavy, stable base that accommodates a magnet-backed glass plate for attaching sandpaper and magnet-backed leather strops for finishing the edge. Each sheet of sandpaper is good for three to five knives before it becomes worn. Even when worn, sandpaper will still sharpen your knives, it just works like a finer grit.

EDGE GUIDES

There are a variety of guide systems available. They clamp onto the spine of the knife and keep your sharpening angle steady throughout the stroke. Edge guides are used with benchstones or waterstones. You use the same motion you would use for freehand sharpening. There are two advantages to using an edge guide. Not only does it keep your angle steady, but is also helps build the proper stroke into muscle memory. Using a guide can improve your freehand sharpening. Because the guide takes up space, you lose a a little usable space on your stone. This is not really a problem if you have a sharpening stone 8 inches or longer.

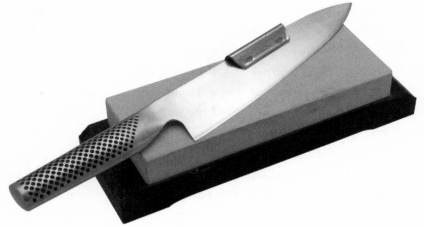

Edge guides clamp onto the spine of the knife to keep the sharpening angle consistent.

The primary disadvantage to using guides is that you are never sure exactly what angle you are grinding into your edge. Knowing the precise angle isn't strictly necessary. Clamp the guide farther back for an acute back bevel and slide it forward for a wider edge angle. If you are trying to achieve exact, repeatable bevels, you can use a felt-tipped marker and the angle finder calculations to adjust the guide so that the spine is at the correct height above the stone. The most popular guides come from Razor Edge Systems. These are well built but require a lot of dexterity to clamp properly. A very inexpensive set of guides—one for larger knives and one for smaller paring knives—is available from MinoSharp. These clamps are easy to use but set an angle between 10 and 15 degrees depending on the width of the knife, and are not easily adjustable for compound bevels.

ROD AND CLAMP SYSTEMS

Rod-guided sharpening systems turn everything upside down. Literally. Rather than gliding the knife over a stone, these sharpening guides slide the stone over the knife. There is a variety of systems available that all work in about the same fashion. The knife is held in a clamp. The stone is attached to a rod. By putting the rod through one of the preset holes in the clamp, you can control the sharpening angle. Available angles range from 10 to 30 degrees, usually in 3- to 5-degree increments. Each system comes with its own set of stones. Double-beveling is very easy with rod-guided sharpening stones. The most common systems are made by Lansky, DMT, and Gatco.

The downside to rod-guided systems is the need to reclamp the knife every couple of inches so the bevel angle doesn't change as you progress from heel to tip. It is also fairly easy to round the tips of your knives on these systems.

The king of the rod-guided systems is the Edge Pro Apex. The Apex is sturdily built and uses relatively large 1- by 6-inch aluminum oxide waterstones that cut very quickly yet leave a high level of polish. The angle guide is continuously adjustable for any angle, with marks at 10, 15, 18, 21, and 25 degrees. Because you don't have to use preset angles, you can set the arm to match any existing edge bevel. The blade rests on a *flat table* rather than being clamped into place. You sweep the stone over a section of the knife about the width of the knife rest, then simply slide the knife over a little to reach the next section. Keeping the edge perpendicular to the stone involves nothing more than turning your wrist a little as the blade narrows toward the tip. Using the Edge Pro allows you to put a scary sharp edge on your knives in a very short amount of time. Be careful, the blade table can harbor runoff grit and metal shavings, which will scratch the blade unless you tape it with painters' tape.

The only downside to the Edge Pro Apex is its cost. This is a professional-level sharpening system, but at $185 for the full kit, it is a little outside the realm of what the average home sharpener is willing to spend. That aside, there is no faster, easier way for someone without a lot of freehand sharpening experience to put a keen, highly polished edge on their knives.

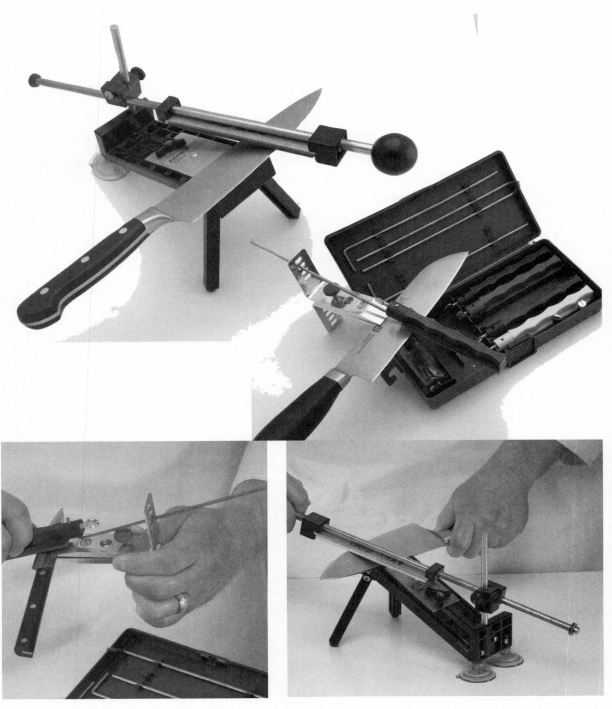

Rod-style systems stroke the stone over the knife at a set angle. Some systems clamp onto the spine of the knife, which makes them difficult to use for large kitchen knives because you have to adjust the clamp as you move down the length of the knife. They are better for paring knives and pocket knives. The Edge Pro Apex allows you to slide the knife along the table to sharpen each section of the knife.

V-SYSTEMS AND CROCK STICKS

V-type sharpeners have two ceramic rods that are placed into a plastic or wooden base at a preset angle. The knife is held perpendicular to the ground and stroked down the rod. Because you hold the knife in a natural position, these systems are fairly easy to use. You just stroke straight up and down. Some variation on a ceramic V-system is available at every hardware and sporting goods store in the country.

The best of the V-systems is the Spyderco Sharpmaker 204. The Sharpmaker solves the two basic problems that plague all crock stick setups, wide angles and round stones. It is difficult to produce a flat edge with a round stone. Round is fine for steels and honing rods because you are realigning the edge, not trying to create a new one. The Sharpmaker uses triangular ceramic rods in medium and fine grits. The angles are preset for performance edges. You don't have to guess, just hold the knife straight up and down and stroke it down the stones. There are two angle settings, 30 and 40, corresponding to 15 degrees and 20 degrees per side, so creating a 15/20 compound edge is nearly foolproof. And, unlike just about anything else out there, you can sharpen serrated knives. It comes with an excellent manual and a video to help get you started. The Sharpmaker is compact and fits neatly into a plastic case, so it is easy to keep handy in the kitchen for quick touch-ups, taking the place of a steel.

There are two downsides to the Sharpmaker. It is easy to glide the knife off the honing rod, especially while using the corners of the rods. This will eventually round the tip of your knife. This is easily remedied by taking your time and sharpening in two stages, one for 90 percent of the edge and a second stage concentrating on the tip only. The other downside is that major reprofiling can take a while. The medium stones are not designed to remove a lot of metal in a hurry. The Sharpmaker is better at keeping your knives at

peak performance than it is putting a radically thinner edge on a thick knife.

PULL-THROUGH SYSTEMS

There are a number of gadgets with tungsten carbide bits or carbide wheels that you draw the knife through, scraping off slivers of steel. Most of these things are not fit to sharpen your lawnmower blades much less your fine kitchen knives. Avoid them. Some pull-through sharpeners have ceramic wheels. These don't do too much damage and can be used for quick touch-ups, but they are not suitable for actual sharpening.

ELECTRIC SHARPENERS

Please promise me that you will never use the knife sharpener on the back of your electric can opener. Please? Electric sharpeners grind very aggressively and can remove a lot of metal in a hurry. You can turn your chef's knife into a filet knife with just a little inattention. Using a bad electric knife sharpener is just about the worst thing you can do to your knives. Poor electric sharpeners have given the entire genre a bad name.

Chef's Choice makes a number of well-designed electric sharpeners. They use multiple stages to create a compound bevel. The Model 120, for example, has three stages, each at a slightly steeper angle. The third stage is a set of flexible stropping disks that will put a reasonably fine polish on your edge. The nice thing about the polishing stage is that it can be used in place of a steel or honing rod and will keep your knives sharp for a very long time. The Model 130 also has a stropping stage. If you have neither the time nor the inclination to sharpen your knives by hand, the Chef's Choice Model 120 or 130 would be a good addition to your kitchen, though the 46-degree total angle (23 degrees per side) the Chef's Choice sharpeners finish with is wider than it should be. The Model

316 sharpener, designed for thinner Japanese-made knives, sharpens to a 15-degree edge angle.

As with all electric sharpening systems, there are things to be aware of. Read the manual. Twice. Do not assume that because the sharpener has three stages you should use all three of them. The first stage cuts very aggressively. It removes metal at a frightening rate. The first stage on Chef's Choice sharpeners comes with a plastic cover on it—for a good reason. It should probably be welded shut and only be made accessible with a notarized affidavit that you have read the manual. Twice. The first stage should only be used if a knife is so dull that it is otherwise unrecoverable, and should only be used once or twice in the life of a knife, not every time you sharpen.

One of the most common problems that professional knife sharpeners encounter is knives ruined by overgrinding on an electric sharpener. The culprit is the bolster. The thick bolster on German and French-style knives changes the angle of the blade against the abrasive wheels of the sharpener, grinding in a hollow spot. This can happen with any sharpening system, but it happens very quickly with overuse of an electric sharpener. Over time, this hollow spot, called a swale, is ground farther than the rest of the edge, preventing the heel of the knife from making full contact with the cutting board. The back half of the knife is now useless. Use the finest stage of an electric sharpener until it is no longer effective, then go to the next lower stage. Use the coarsest stage only as a last resort.

PROFESSIONAL KNIFE SHARPENING

If you've read this far, you *are* a sharpening professional.

If you want to send your knives out to be sharpened, that's fine, but remember, finding a good sharpener is like finding someone to cut your hair. It's somewhat hit or miss. Just because someone has a sign on the door and a grinder in the back doesn't mean that you'll get exactly what you were expecting.

If you have a cutlery store or specialty gourmet store nearby, they may offer sharpening services. You are now an informed consumer. Ask questions. Will they sharpen to specific angles? Do they charge extra for a back bevel? Are they willing to grind a 15/20 or 10/15 compound bevel that you can touch up yourself? What grit do they finish the edge with? Are they willing to put a fine polish on your edges? If you don't get answers you like, go elsewhere. You can do much better than a part-time employee with a knife-sharpening machine.

If you are looking for a good professional sharpener, ask your hairstylist. Hair shears are even more expensive and esoteric than the priciest knives. If your barber or stylist is happy with the person who sharpens their shears, that person will probably do an excellent job with your kitchen knives. You could also ask the chef of a nice restaurant who sharpens his knives. Many restaurants use rental knives that are coarsely sharpened, but the executive chef and sous chefs will have their own knives and will have them sharpened regularly. Find out who they use.

If you can't find a local sharpener, there are professionals who accept mail-order sharpening. The experts at Epicurean Edge, Korin, and The Kitchen Drawer (see Resources) all do excellent work. Call or e-mail them for current pricing and shipping instructions. For a real treat, send your knives to one of the best in the business, Dave Martell at D&R Sharpening in Pennsylvania. Martell specializes in sharpening high-end kitchen knives, including Japanese knives. His standard sharpening service is reasonably priced and puts an astounding edge on your knives. If you are after the ultimate edge, Martell offers an upper-tier service—hand finished on Japanese waterstones and leather hones—that has chefs around the country lining up at their mailboxes.

CONCLUSION

There you have it. The veil has been lifted and you can see that the man behind the curtain really doesn't have anything special going for him. This is stuff that anyone can do with a little practice. Do not ever let anyone tell you that good knife skills or sharpening are too hard or too complicated. Most recipes could be viewed in exactly the same way. They're complicated. They require specialized knowledge and technique. They're a little scary. So what? You'd be insulted if someone told you that a particular dish was beyond your abilities. At the very least you'd be righteously indignant. You should feel the same way the next time you are hesitant about dicing an onion or if someone suggests that you send your knives to a professional for sharpening. Good knife skills are simply a matter of patience and practice. If you can cook, you can sharpen. Just remember the basics—angle, abrasive, consistency, and burr. And just like cooking, you become better and better by doing. Your first attempt might not be perfect. But it *will* be your achievement. No one else's. And it just gets better after that.

RESOURCES

A. G. Russell Knives
2900 South 26th Street
Rogers, AR 72758-8571
800-255-9034
ag@agrussell.com
www.agrussell.com
Great kitchen knives and accessories since 1964

Benchcrafted
www.benchcrafted.com
info@benchcrafted.com
Makers of beautiful furniture grade Mag-Blok magnetic knife bars

Big Tray Restaurant Equipment
1200 7th Street
San Francisco, CA 94107
800-BIG-TRAY (244-8729)
help@bigtray.com
www.bigtray.com
Good deals on restaurant supplies. One of the few places to find
the Sani-Tuff rubber cutting boards

The Board Smith
David Smith
High Point, NC
boardsmith@triad.rr.com
336-803-0434
www.theboardsmith.com
Gorgeous handcrafted cutting boards from a woodworker and furniture maker with 45 years' experience

Broadway Panhandler
65 East 8th Street
New York, NY 10003
866-266-5927
bpisales@broadwaypanhandler.com
www.broadwaypanhandler.com
One of New York's finest kitchenwares stores. Owner Norman Kornbluth knows his knives.

Butcher & Packer
1468 Gratiot Avenue
Detroit, MI 48207
800-521-3188
al@butcher-packer.com
www.butcher-packer.com
Forschners chef's knives, cutting boards, sausage-making supplies

Chef Depot
630-739-5200
chefdepot@yahoo.com
www.chefdepot.net
Online retailer of cutlery (including Messermeister knives), cutting boards, and kitchen tools

Cooking.com

2850 Ocean Park Boulevard, Suite 310

Santa Monica, CA 90405

800-663-8810

www.cooking.com

Mail-order and online purveyor of cutlery (including Global and Messermeister) and kitchen tools

A Cook's Wares

211 37th Street

Beaver Falls, PA 15010

800-915-9788

sales@cookswares.com

www.cookswares.com

Knowledgeable retailer of cutlery (including MAC and Messermeister), cutting boards, kitchen tools, and appliances

D&R Sharpening Solutions

Dave Martell

789 DeLong Road

Alburtis, PA 18011

215-350-3445

DRmailbox@drsharpening.com

www.drsharpening.com

Dave Martell is one of the best professional sharpeners in the business. His mail-order sharpening service is the secret weapon of many professional chefs.

Edge Pro Inc.

P.O. Box 95

Hood River, OR 97031

541-387-2222

edgepro@gorge.net

www.edgeproinc.com

Makers of the Edge Pro Apex sharpening system, the best of the guided sharpening rigs

Epicurean Edge

107 Central Way

Kirkland, WA 98033

425-889-5980

info@bladegallery.com

www.epicedge.com

Epicurean Edge/Blade Gallery is Knife Mecca West, home to one of the largest selections of high-end kitchen knives anywhere. Owner Daniel O'Malley is extremely knowledgeable about kitchen knives and knives in general. Sister Web site Blade Gallery (www.bladegallery.com) frequently carries custom kitchen knives, including those from Thomas Haslinger.

Fante's Kitchen Wares

1006 South Ninth Street

Philadelphia, PA 19147-4798

800-44-FANTE (32683)

mail@fantes.com

www.fantes.com

Knives and kitchenwares since 1906. Huge selection and lots of information

HandAmerican

P.O. Box 902

South Plainfield, NJ 07080-0902

888-819-6196

info@handamerican.com

www.handamerican.com

The best source for leather strops, honing compounds, sandpaper-based sharpening systems, and smooth steels

Japanese Chef's Knife

1803-5 Oze, Seki City

Gifu, Japan 501-3265

81-575-38-3019

koki@kencrest.us

www.japanesechefsknife.com

Do not let ordering from Japan scare you. This Japanese knife exporter is truly wonderful to deal with. They have an excellent selection, reasonable prices, and startlingly fast shipping. Orders take only 3 to 5 days to reach a U.S. address. One of the best sources for Japanese-made Western-style knives

The Japan Chef

1731 Clement Avenue

Alameda, CA 94501

888-537-7820

support@thejapanchef.com

www.thejapanchef.com

Sister site of www.japanwoodworker.com, The Japan Chef specializes in Japanese-made kitchen knives and sharpening tools.

Kitchen Drawer

4068 Albany Post Road

Hyde Park, NY 12538

845-229-2300

thekitchendrawer@verizon.net

Owner Erin Griffin really knows his knives. Located near the Culinary Institute of America, The Kitchen Drawer supplies students and teaching chefs with quality cutlery and kitchen gear.

The Knife Merchant

4740 Garfield Street

La Mesa, CA 91941

800-714-8226

sales@knifemerchant.com

www.knifemerchant.com

Chef John Borg brings forty years of professional kitchen experience to his online store, stocking knives from the inexpensive Forschner line through the ultra high-end Nenox knives. The Knife Merchant also sells cutting boards and kitchen tools.

Knife Outlet

66400 Oak Road

Lakeville, IN 46536

800-607-9948

info@knifeoutlet.com

www.knifeoutlet.com

Owner Fred Whitlock is passionate about kitchen knives and sells MAC, Messermeister, and Kikuichi knives and Edge Pro sharpening systems in addition to the more common lines of cutlery.

Korin

57 Warren Street

New York, NY 10007

800-626-2172

sales@korin.com

www.korin.com

Knife Mecca East. Marketed primarily toward professional chefs, Korin offers a vast array of traditional Japanese and Japanese-made Western-style knives, sharpening stones, and sharpening services. If you are looking for anything from a basic starter knife to a $3,000 custom-forged sushi knife, Korin probably has it in stock.

Lee Valley Tools

Multiple locations throughout Canada

800-871-8158

customerservice@leevalley.com

www.leevalley.com

Purveyor of fine woodworking and gardening tools along with an exceptional assortment of sharpening tools, waterstones, oil stones, and just plain nifty stuff

Michigan Maple

P.O. Box 245

Petoskey, MI 49770

231-347-4170

mmb@mapleblock.com

www.mapleblock.com

Michigan Maple is one of the original inventors of the end-grain butcher block and has been making and selling them for more than 100 years. Some products can be purchased directly through their Web site; others must be purchased through retail vendors.

1sharpknife.com

1416 Silver Saddle NE

Albuquerque, NM 87113

sales@1sharpknife.com

www.1sharpknife.com

Well-regarded mail-order sharpening service that also sells the Edge Pro Apex sharpening system and the truly excellent Idahone ceramic honing rods

Professional Cutlery Direct/Cooking Enthusiast
242 Branford Road
North Branford, CT 06471
800-792-6650
info@cutlery.com
www.cutlery.com
Well-stocked kitchen gear and cutlery store. Carries Forschner/
Victorinox and Global in addition to standard knives

Shapton USA
51 Shattuck Street
Pepperell, MA 01463
877-692-3624
hms@japanesetools.com
www.shaptonstones.com
Home of the spectacular Shapton Professional and GlassStone
Japanese waterstones

Sharpening Supplies.com
313 West Beltline Highway, Suite 49
Madison, WI 53713
800-351-8234
customerservice@sharpeningsupplies.com
www.sharpeningsupplies.com
Sharpening gear, books, online tutorials, and more

Tools for Working Wood
32 33rd Street, 5th floor
Brooklyn, NY 11232
800-426-4613
support@toolsforworkingwood.com
www.toolsforworkingwood.com
Waterstones, oil stones, abrasive films, and other sharpening
equipment

ACKNOWLEDGMENTS

First (and always) I need to thank my wife, Lisa, and my kids, Sarah and Jack. They were amazing (and amazingly patient).

As you might imagine, I had to pester a lot of people to pull this much information together. I especially appreciate Sara Moulton, Masaharu Morimoto, Russ Parsons, Michael Ruhlman, and Martin Yan for taking time out of their busy schedules to answer my questions. Dr. Dean O. Cliver and Dr. Peter Snyder helped me grasp the intricacies of microbiology and cutting board sanitation. Others I need to thank include chef Douglas Pitts, Marsha Lynch, Ron Beck and Neil Horwitz at Beck's Cutlery in Cary, North Carolina, and the good folks of Knifeforums.com's "In the Kitchen" forum, the one place, even in the weird world of the Internet, where owning 43 chef's knives is not particularly unusual. Thanks to Lee, Curtis, Shawn, Ken, Fish, Pam, Brandon, Bob, Ed, Thom, Joe, Chad, Jered, Bert, Andy, Larrin, Nick, Curt, Mike, John, Zini, and Jim. Special thanks also to Dave Martell at D&R Sharpening for always being willing to discuss the far reaches of knife sharpening and Warren Prince for his extraordinary generosity. There are fewer than 100 certified Master Bladesmiths in the world. I had three of them who shared their time and insights with me: thanks to Murray Carter, Bob Kramer, and Kevin Cashen for their help.

This whole project would not have happened had it not

been for my agent, Helena Schwarz, and my editors Harriet Bell and Gail Winston, along with the team at William Morrow: Sarah Whitman-Salkin, David Sweeney, Cassie Jones, Dee Dee DeBartolo, Aryana Hendrawan, Ann Cahn, Lorie Pagnozzi, Tavia Kowalchuk, James B. Houston, Allison Saltzman, Mary Ann Petyak, and my copyeditor Suzanne Fass.

INDEX

Note: **Boldfaced** page references refer to color insert pages.

Messermeister knives, 22, 46, 61, 71, 72–74, 75, 76, 78

Mick Jagger Trick, **Color Plate 31**

mincing garlic, **Color Plates 22–23**

mincing technique, **Color Plates 12–13**

MinoSharp edge guides, 202

molybdenum, 33, 34

Mouse Pad Trick, 159, 160–61

N

nakiri knife, 44, 63–64

newsprint, slicing, 185

nickel, 33

Nogent knives, 80

Norton stones, 162, 200

O

oblique (roll) cut, **Color Plate 16**

offset bread knife, 60

onions, dicing, **Color Plates 18–21**

onions, slicing, tips for, **Color Plate 21**

online shopping sites, 28, 67–68, 80

P

Paper Airplane Trick, 149

paring knives

budget-priced, 70

description of, 53–54

Forschner/Victorinox, 69

MAC, 70–71

Messermeister, 71

Shun, 74

versatility of, 11

Wüsthof-Trident, 71

patina, 38

paysanne cut, **Color Plate 17**

peelers, 65–66

peppers, preparing, **Color Plates 28–29**

petty knife, 45, 54

phosphorus, 33

the Pinch (grip), 27, 109–10, **Color Plate 2**

planks, cutting, **Color Plate 3**

plastic (poly) cutting boards, 88, 90–91, 93

potatoes

Potato Leek Soup, 117–20

Shoestring Fries, 127–29

professional knife sharpening, 207–8

PSA-backed sandpaper, 159, 160, 201

pull-through sharpeners, 206

pull-through steels, 151

push cuts, 111–12

Q

quarter-roll trick, **Color Plates 20–21**

R

Razor Edge Systems, 152, 202

recipes

Chicken under a Brick (Pollo al Mattone), 123–24

Julienned Vegetables, 113–14

Potato Leek Soup, 117–20

Salmon Two Ways, 125–26

Shoestring Fries, 127–29

Summer Lentil Salad, 115–16

"relaxation effect," 152

Richlite cutting boards, 89, 93

rivets, 27

Rockwell C scale, 30, 135